Writing Pauline

Wisdom from a Long Life

Gail J. Stearns

Hamilton Books
an imprint of
UNIVERSITY PRESS OF AMERICA,® INC.
Lanham • Boulder • New York • Toronto • Oxford

Copyright © 2005 by
Hamilton Books
4501 Forbes Boulevard
Suite 200
Lanham, Maryland 20706
UPA Acquisitions Department (301) 459-3366

PO Box 317
Oxford
OX2 9RU, UK

Library of Congress Control Number: 2005926919
ISBN 0-7618-3121-5 (paperback : alk. ppr.)

To Jeana and John

Contents

Figures

Not only is it important to honor a life well lived, but it is equally as important to view a personal history—to understand the intersection of personal decisions and public events, the circuitous paths of reality, and true discovery versus mere repetition. It may be humbling to realize that we are not the first to have done, seen, said, thought, decided. However, without the historical knowledge there are no real insights.

Jo Hockenhull, Washington State University, 1994

Preface

I have just received Gail Stearns' biography of me. And I am both astounded and delighted. I had not known that she was doing any writing at all, and had completely written off the whole writing project initiated by the Women's Studies Department of Washington State University some five years ago. It was an accident actually that a biography of me was thought to be the best way to implement the use of my biographical material which had been put into the WSU archives. . . . [After several years of little contact] I simply wrote the whole idea off.

Then out of the blue arrived this manuscript, complete, ready for an editor [and] publisher.

So I began reading it in a very skeptical frame of mind. I had begun to wonder if *any*one could understand the profound changes and (as I felt) spiritual development that had been taking place in me after a physical accident precipitated my leaving the project.

At the same time as all these fundamental changes within my own personal life, I was perceiving the world situation—the cosmos—our cosmos—this planet—to be undergoing equally new consciousness and attitude and direction and history, the same total mystery as my individual one—fantastically multiplied quantitatively. I am just one grain of sand on a beach full of sand—the external eye not different from any other grain of sand—to find that with the inner eye I can be seen as entirely different from any other grain of sand in all times and all places. I went from that incredible and startling discovery to the realization that to that same inner eye all of us grains of sand are basically distinguishable from each other. I think Tennyson is the one who said it: to a primrose . . . "if I could know this root and branch and all I would know who God and man. . . ."

As I have pursued this new path of experience in this way, this Tao, I find that the main influence of my adult life has become the study of the psychology of Carl Jung. I remember a history course I once took during which we debated Carlisle's concept that history is the study of the lives of great men. This definition was countered by the contrary proposition that history was written by the unconscious influence of the collective world. I think the main thrust of my own attitude is best represented by a book [written by several professors at Columbia] who said, "All Knowledge is Additive." Tennyson said the same thing: "I am a part of all that I have met." These two aphorisms amount to the same thing, and they summarize a whole new attitude toward human life. More vision in our century than in the countless preceding millennium.

So with this final stage of my long, full life, I find myself constrained by the necessity of trying to make relevant and unexpected intelligible reference to a new character and a new role in my life history. And to my stunned surprise Gail seems to me to have caught the woman I now am. She accepts—it seems to me at the moment at least—that what I am perceiving is a change of psychological type. I used to say laughingly that I was having such a happy old age because my early age was lived by my "inferior function." I did my homework before I took the course. The structure of our society led me to believe that doctors were scientists and that scientists should eliminate emotion, feeling, and personal involvement. Actually I spent all of my time and libido trying to be a scientist. School—grades—courses—assignments—promotions—I was an egghead and a square and an opinionated prig. (Prig is such an ancient word, almost a Jane Austen word.) I was a prig and I approved of prigs. It's no wonder my sex life wound up on the rocks. I did not know that unconsciously I was deliberately making it like that. One of my longtime friends—from exactly fifty years ago in fact—has become a world's specialist in Jungian circles on the topic of psychological types and he still thinks that our basic types don't change. Well, mine seems to have changed.

As Gail writes my life, to me she seems unquestionably to see me as an introvert. I now see my role as testifying to "that inward eye which is the bliss of solitude." Of course, maybe [my friend] Wayne is quite right; that is to say that maybe I was living primarily on my inferior function for the first quarter of my life, and in struggle, conflict and confusion for the half of my life that followed. The final quarter of thought had culminated in a resolution of this conflict. Again a Christian and a vastly different Christian from my childhood. The quarternating God is a different image from the Trinitarian God of the usual New Testament. And now to my total surprise this coda . . . [of the quaternating God is] crowning, more mature, more brightly, clearly visible and almost tangible—*whole* Christian [as in] "and you shall see the truth, and the truth will make you free."

And I feel that Gail has seen and understood *this change*. My new road.

When Gail sent me her manuscript, she asked if I would give some feedback. What I have now written may not seem like feedback but it is. I am deeply touched right down to the core with an amazed perception that here is a woman who almost solely on the data provided in the archives was able to find an unexpected wholeness in the life I have lived. My essentially religious nature has unconsciously dominated my whole existence. All those middle years of loneliness and personal abandonment by a God who supposedly gave direction to one's life—and I a grown woman still wanting to be mother's good little girl and breaking mother's heart instead, feeling not only unredeemed but unredeemable—no wonder I have found old age delightful.

And no wonder just last week was one of the *worst* weeks in my life, for that is when Gail's manuscript came and helped convert the worst week of all to the latest best insight of all.

Everything went wrong last week. I won't bother to enumerate. It touched everything. It even included the unexpected death of my only remaining close relative. It was winding up with a profound consciousness that "the world that I had loved so much had turned to dust and ashes at my touch." I did not have a "support group" any more. They had scattered all over the globe, one friend in Australia, two in Europe, one in Mexico, one in Arizona, etc., two "passed away" (an evasion I particularly dislike). In short I did not feel loved.

And with that came the latest lesson of my new life: You can't develop—you *can't* progress if you don't feel loved. I repeat: you can't develop if you don't feel loved.

If we let this third path be our guide to conduct it simplifies everything incredibly. I have proclaimed for years that "Love is the answer." After last week I know that love is only half the answer. Feeling oneself *being loved* is the other essential half of the answer.

This business of Christians being humble and lowly is a TRAGIC error of our thinking. . . . At last are *three* roads ahead—yang: too long too conservative and prohibitive, as in "Thou shalt not. . . ." Yin: too weak and irresponsible and uncertain, too weak and undeveloped and timid and fearful and passive, our values too earthbound, not realized. Lazy? Selfish? Trivial? Weak feminine, not earth-mother, nurturing, loving feminine.

The new third way. Transcendent feminine: a complete, whole square/round genuinely three-dimensional word. Serving Heaven as our unattainable goal, it is enough that we keep—and *can* keep—our direction—our balance and harmony, our inspiration and expiration, our left foot/right foot; hay foot/straw foot Tao making a full progress through a loving, loved life.

If we seek a new road of love instead of continuing to overbalance in the old world of thought, of the male Trinity, then we know that we don't misuse the funds by donating to upgrade our retirement hospital wards at Laguna Honda into four-bed wards; we know that we don't tear down an old prison and then build one even more imprisoning; we know that we don't turn a playground into a parking lot; we know that we don't cut the school lunch program; we know that we don't set up commissions to plan how to spend our surplus at the same time we have homeless walking the streets. We don't assert a trickle-down theory of economics. (If we were properly loving, we would never *have* a body of homeless citizens and simultaneously have surplus income to begin with.)

So my surprised feedback to Gail's work is an immense gratitude for her beautiful depiction of my life. I would never have been so lost if she had not given me the fuel, as it were, to see life more deeply. To admit and to contend and to recognize my own sense of failure and at the same time to assert my own success. I now feel an even greater certainty that I have finally become a "successful failure". . . .[1] I realize that "greater certainty" is perhaps an oxymoron (I never did really cope with this word. It wasn't certainty if I now have more certainty?).

Maybe I'm saying that I'll have other attacks of doubt about life on earth and/or self-doubt, but I *know* now in a new way—and remember that I am 94 years old now and moreover feeling my age for the first time—I feel again and more deeply still that I know that "Love is the answer" even if it proves to be unsuccessful, better to be an unsuccessful lover than to attain power. And, moreover, I know that I am loved. And I know that I love you, and I know that you love me. Thank you.

                                        Pauline E. Thompson, San Francisco, July 1999

Acknowledgments

I thank two former directors of Women's Studies at Washington State University, Jo Hockenhull, Emeritus Professor of Fine Arts, and Sue Armitage, Professor of History, who invited me to take on the writing of Pauline's life and provided comments on early drafts. Noël Sturgeon, current Chair of the Women's Studies Department, has continued the involvement of Women's Studies in this project. I thank each of them for their support and their friendship throughout. I am grateful to Laila Miletic-Vejzovic, Head of Manuscripts, Archives, and Special Collections at WSU who has offered every available resource in the use of the Pauline Thompson collection. In addition, I thank Dan Peterson, Senior Vice President of University Advancement at WSU for his assistance in seeing the project through to publication.

I owe a great deal of appreciation to Karen Weathermon for many hours of careful editing and helpful suggestions for the book, and to Valerie McIlroy, Jungian Analyst, for sharing her expertise. I offer Carol Brownson, Pauline's goddaughter and executor many thanks for her willing cooperation throughout this process and for experiencing with me Pauline's interventions and comments on the progress of this project. I am grateful to many WSU students who have shared my enthusiasm for Pauline's theology and stirred my writing with stimulating conversations.

Finally, my family has been part of this process from the beginning. Pauline recognized and delighted in my son John's "soul journey" early on when she stayed in Pullman and when John and I met her for interviews in San Francisco. My spouse, Tim Moody, enjoyed conversations with Pauline when she visited our home, and both he and my daughter, Jeana, have been with me throughout these hours of writing Pauline. Thank you.

Copyright permissions are granted by Carol P. Brownson for poetry by Margaret Truesdale Gibbs and for interviews, conversations, photographs, letters, and writings by Pauline E. Thompson; and by Manuscripts, Archives, and Special Collections of Washington State University for sketches and contents of the Pauline E. Thompson Papers, Cage 676. Interviews, writings, and emails from Kay Anderson, Carol Brownson, David Hartsough, Jo Hockenhull, Robert Levering, and Liza Rognes used by permission.

Introduction

Pauline Thompson was an extraordinary character. Not a well-known person, she was a woman of remarkable wisdom. Her views on politics, religion, aging, and women were well ahead of her time. Yet, as I learned stories of her life, I sensed incongruence between the foolishness of her youth and the depth of perception she achieved in old age. In the 1930s and 40s Pauline listlessly engaged in pointless love affairs and held countless professional positions. By the 1990s she lived and wrote with poignancy and rare wisdom. In January 1993 she wrote that after many years she realized, "It is as if I had been stumbling and falling all my life, consciously off-course, without even knowing there was a course."[1] In September of the same year she concluded that, like God, "we, too, must create; we too must extract heaven from the Chaos into which we are born. That is our meaning, our task, and should be our *joy*."[2] How did she make this remarkable shift, from a life of chaos to uncommon wisdom?

I first met Pauline when she visited Washington State University to accept a Women's Studies Lifetime Achievement Award in 1994. Pauline was eighty-seven years old. She appeared frail, colorless, and petite, wearing a large white neck brace that encumbered her movements and a gray polyester pantsuit; her gray hair was swept back behind her neck without a care, and she had pale gray-blue eyes. Yet her appearance belied her personality. Feisty, opinionated, generous, intelligent, passionate, Pauline posed a challenge to academics, friends and activists at every turn.

Later, as I returned home from a memorial service for Pauline Thompson at the San Francisco Society of Friends House in January 2001, I was more fully conscious of the reason I felt driven to engage in ethnographic work on her life ever since I met her. Having known Pauline meant my life and views would never be the same.

Hers was a moral and spiritual life filled with irony and complexity—beginning with a strict Methodist upbringing, subsequently including a deconversion to atheism and Communist leanings for over forty years, political activism (Pauline was last arrested for sitting-in at a nuclear facility at the age of ninety-four), delving into Quakerism and Jungianism, and eventually a reconversion to Christianity. Throughout the twentieth century Pauline had careers as varied as the years through which she lived. She was a teacher of mentally disabled and blind children, teacher and drama coach of privileged private-school children, nurse for migrant workers, World War II veteran, psychiatric nurse, Jungian analysand and psychologist, and Doctor of Education. She had love affairs equally varied, with both women and men.

Embedded in this life history are questions and unfolding answers concerning how Pauline made the shift from foolishness to wisdom. Her life is presented first as biography, including Pauline's reflections upon that life story. Once her story is told, the theology Pauline developed in late life is described more explicitly (chapter six). Finally, connections are drawn between Pauline's philosophy and theology and contemporary theory on subjects including psychology, religion, ethics, and ethnography (chapter seven). Pauline's is a story that is deeply self-reflective, and a story that challenges even our smallest notions of human behavior and ethics. Pauline's views and experience add intriguing twists, for example, to women's rights and ideas of the feminine. Abortion is permissible, she held, but her primary justification was one previously unimagined in my study of feminist theory. Marriage is critical—the only truly moral choice for women, she thought. Yet she experienced and learned from everything but marriage, including relationships that were bigamous, passionate, and both male and female centered.

Pauline's life and ideas challenge developmental theories of what it means to be an ethical or moral person, belying Christian and psychological understandings alike. The theology she developed in her later years offers a unique alternative to that found in ordinary church theology. Likewise, her character offers distinctive challenges to traditional theories of what it means to be fully moral.

Pauline's growth throughout the years even calls into question the very theory to which she devoted the last half of her life—that of Carl Jung. As she aged, Pauline increasingly reflected upon the collective meaning of both conscious events and a collective unconscious. An event that occurred at age thirteen was recalled by Pauline at age eighty-five because she finally understood why it had reappeared in a drawing she had sketched at age fifty. Pauline's memories themselves were remarkable—telling the life of an independent woman who lived throughout the socially tormented and technologically successful twentieth century. Her memories took on greater significance as their meaning emerged for her after nearly ten decades. And while upholding Jung's theories, ironically Pauline's life changes and complex personality led her to go against mainstream Jungian thought and to question the stasis of personality types.

Finally, ethnographic work on Pauline's life brings new insight to issues regarding objectivity in research. Because she perpetually brought newness and change into the lives of those around her, including that of the ethnographer, studying her life story challenges traditional anthropological notions of subjectivity in research.

Pauline offers challenge not only to current ideas, but to the way we think and live our lives. In her, we encounter new insights into spirituality, synchronicity, symbolism, the feminine, faith, and fullness of life. Throughout the process of writing her life, unexplainable experiences permeated Pauline's world and marked my time with her. One of those was a sense of being outside of time, in a space of recollection and meaning—the experience of time standing still. I recall one day arriving at Pauline's doorstep near lunchtime, bringing lunch to share from a local deli so she would not need to dig out one of the many meals-on-wheels she had stashed into her refrigerator. We sat at Pauline's old kitchen table, and I turned on my tape recorder and began our interview. The air soon filled with Pauline's stories, remarkably varied, yet all connected in some way—from the plight of elephants in Africa to the current state of the U.S. presidency. On one level I listened to Pauline articulate a unique definition of ethics, and on another watched her lunch grow cold ("I'll eat it later," Pauline commented). Carrying steaming cups of Pauline's favorite ginseng tea we retired to the worn, brown couch in the living room, talking until the light grew a pale gray as the sun slipped below the horizon. ("She never turned on a light, you know," a friend of Pauline's once noted.) I was quite startled when I glanced at my watch and realized not one, as I had thought, but five hours had elapsed. Time was temporarily suspended as I entered Pauline's world of story, presence, and thought.

I have little doubt that had any reader known her in the last decade of the twentieth century Pauline would have invited him or her into her kitchen to share a meal. And if she felt a connection with such a person, the day would escape, unnoticed, until the sun slipped beneath the horizon. It is my hope that Pauline's spirit will continue to teach us through her words and story.

Figure 1.	Sketch of Pauline E. Thompson at a Quaker meeting, Spring 1985

Chapter One

Childhood and Character

Pauline's Story
I went one night to a field to lie down in a furrow,
to cry there and sleep in the only place I could be.
The dry ploughed earth took the seed of my tears
and my hurt went deep to the rich dark loam of the land
to be lost away from me. Nobody saw when I left the house
and my straightened bed that was soft and square
and gave me no room to rest in the grain of my grief.
But the furrow lay long and was open to me
where I put my face in the dirt. The strong black smell
of the summer land came cool in my throat and my hands
uncurled. My full length stretched till the soil
gave way to the shape I was, and let me stay.
There's no like place in the city and now I can't
even tell so you know what I mean:
how quiet the night on the ground, how the stars
came down from the sky to cover and comfort me.

Jeanne Lohmann, San Francisco, 1983

Pauline once wrote that she did not believe one could be a Christian without embracing paradox. Likewise, one cannot understand Pauline without acknowledging paradox. As an elder woman, and one suspects similarly throughout her life, Pauline left a person with one of two immediate impressions, each in its way equally legitimate. Either one felt Pauline had lost her mind, or at least simply talked too much, and he or she could not get away soon enough, or one sensed she was a wise elder and was eager for further conversation with her. Pauline recognized this irony and noted that, during a

1

hospital visit late in her life, one nurse treated her as though she was a "batty old woman," whereas another stated that Pauline was the "wisest woman" she had ever met. Pauline received both reactions as well during a temporary residence at Friends House, a Quaker retirement home north of San Francisco in the last decade of her life.

In late May, 1997 in her bungalow at Friends House I conducted my first prolonged series of interviews with Pauline. At that time I caught my first glimmer of Pauline's simultaneous self-absorption and her deeply thoughtful, infectious character.[1]

In the spring of 1997, Pauline temporarily moved out of her home in the heart of San Francisco, a home located two blocks from the Presidio and just a few more blocks from the Golden Gate Bridge. Pauline had resided in this row house since 1967. Nearing her ninety-second birthday, and recovering from a difficult bout with pneumonia, she felt it was time to move into a retirement center with facilities that could accommodate any illness she might encounter as she continued to age. Years before, Pauline had given money to help start Friends House in Santa Rosa, California. By 1997 her contribution, which had to her seemed an amount large enough initially to get the center off the ground, amounted simply to an early deposit (at a significantly reduced rate) for a home should she herself plan to retire there.[2]

Susan, a manager and resident social worker of Friends House, indicated the mixed impressions Pauline left. She discussed how frustrating it could be to get an answer from Pauline. She noted that when she had just five minutes Pauline was very hard to pin down. She would make up her mind only to change it later that very day. Susan admitted, however, that even having known Pauline for only six weeks she had come to see she was a remarkable woman for her age. She had never known anyone quite like her.

Mike, executive manager of Friends House, was more reflective as we talked about Pauline. She was independently minded, but that was part of being a Quaker, he said, adding there were many such residents at Friends House. He acknowledged she must have been disappointed in what she found there. She had known Elizabeth, one of the women whose initial vision and work were central in the formation of Friends House, and must have shared her vision. She also must have expected more help, especially as she was recovering from pneumonia. But, he noted, she was in an independent apartment.

Indeed, Pauline was extremely disillusioned with Friends House. She did expect nursing care when she was ill, though it was not a part of her contract at all, as the long-term care center was filled with residents and operated quite apart from the independent residences where Pauline resided.

Although I met some of her neighbors, whom I sensed were filled with a great love of life, and although I witnessed Pauline's genuine pleasure and charming conversation upon meeting them, Pauline's own interests differed from many around her. Paradoxically, she was both too dependent on these independent neighbors, calling upon them for assistance such as a ride to an appointment, and too intellectually and philosophically independent in her thinking to be at home among them.

That Pauline was an intellectual, a dreamer, and a philosopher, thus setting her apart from her (mostly younger) neighbors, was evident as soon as one approached her flat. Notably absent was the familiar flickering of a television that one observed when walking by the majority of the residential units. Each flat at Friends House had a small garden in front for the residents to tend themselves. Unlike many residents, Pauline's priorities during her several month stay clearly resided inside. She was not terribly interested in her garden, but did allow her neighbor to plant bushes and flowers there, as long as they were not so tall as to block her view from her front window. Stepping inside her flat, one's eyes were drawn to the large wooden desk that dominated the center of the front room, separating the kitchen from the living area. The desk was piled and ringed, as was the periphery of the room, with stacks of papers and boxes filled with Pauline's papers, letters, diaries, and books.

Pauline's uniqueness was again revealed in the Friends House directory that Pauline pulled out to show me. Under the heading "Occupations" appeared this list:

Vocation: Librarian, teacher, nurse, Psychologist

Avocation: Environmental concerns; Jungian psychology; political activist

Hobbies: You name it! Metaphysics: Tarot, I Ching, ESP, etc; sewing, cooking, carpentry, gardening, gerontology, travel

Further down the page, under a section entitled "Special in Life," Pauline did not include anything one might expect, such as "friends," or "family." Instead, she wrote at a theologically and spiritually deeper level: "Special in Life: Life itself. Religion (not creed), value and God, not just knowledge — wisdom."[3] One suspects there had never been a biographical entry quite like Pauline's in the Friends House directory.

Pauline had barely recovered from pneumonia when she moved to Friends House in March of 1997. In late June of the same year, Pauline was having some of her possessions shipped between her home in San Francisco and Friends House, when, not satisfied with the way they were situated in the back of a truck, the ninety-two-year-old woman climbed up herself to fix them. She fell off the truck, fracturing her hip. A Veteran of World War II, Pauline was taken to the Veterans Administration Hospital, where she stayed in the long-term care facility for over four months. She was bitterly disappointed that she could not be cared for at Friends House in lieu of the VA Hospital, and vowed not to return to Friends.

Pauline determined on her own to return to her home in San Francisco after lengthy negotiations with Washington State University, by then managing the property as its benefactor. One night, she arranged on her own to catch a bus that would take her from Santa Rosa to her home near the Presidio. She arrived in the latter neighborhood near midnight, and the small, physically frail elder walked by herself a number of blocks to her home. She managed to get inside the basement and fell asleep on an old mattress there. When a representative from the rental agency arrived the next morning, she took Pauline to be a vagrant asleep in the basement. Pauline Evelyn Thompson did not react kindly to such a suggestion.

Until her death three years later, Pauline resided again in the six rooms on the main floor of her San Francisco home. She received meals-on-wheels and, within only months of being released from the VA Hospital, was already on her fourth or fifth visiting nurse. In a tone characteristic of Pauline, who had very high expectations of anyone who promised or was assigned to dealings with her, she claimed this last nurse was "the only one who has done a *thing* for me."[4] Pauline was surrounded by stacks of papers wrapped in twine and piles of books not yet sorted after her recent move. At times, she carefully maneuvered a walker (a complete embarrassment to her) between these items and the furniture. Her couch sat under the front bay window, next to her desk. Across the room, in what was presumably once the dining room, was her bed. Between the bed and couch one tiptoed over a paper collection of some ninety years. The bedroom, at the back of the house, was itself filled with yet unpacked boxes from the move back to her home.

At the foot of Pauline's bed was another desk on which lay a phone surrounded by dozens of scraps of paper containing names and numbers of phone calls received and to be made. Indeed, despite living alone, Pauline did not tend to be alone for long stretches of time. The phone and doorbell rang often, with friends from various walks of life calling to check in on her. On one particular Friday toward the end of November those calls included a meal deliverer who rang the bell, bearing lunch and dinner, a visiting nurse coming by to visit and refill pill boxes, a neighbor dropping by with fresh vegetables, and a masseuse, stopping over to give Pauline a massage and talk about herbal remedies for her various ailments. In the midst of this activity caused by living persons and surrounded by the written words of the past, Pauline reminisced, during the hour or two stretches between interruptions, about her childhood.

CHILDHOOD

Pauline was born March 7, 1905, in Spokane, Washington. Her mother, Ida (Paul) Thompson, was one of thirteen children, and one of two daughters who was sent to college in Willamette, Washington. Ida worked nearly all of her adult life, in addition to caring for her elderly mother and sister and raising two children, Pauline and her older brother, Rex, eventually as a single parent. Pauline's father, Edward, was a professor, teacher, real estate broker, and builder who played a central role in Pauline's life until he left the family in Pauline's twelfth year.

Both Ida and Edward were educators, and in 1905 were teaching at Northwest Business College in Spokane. That year, the owner sold the college, and Edward seems to have left his employment shortly thereafter. It is likely that he did not see eye to eye with his new employer, a circumstance he would encounter in subsequent positions as well. At the time of Pauline's birth in March of 1905, Edward found work selling real estate, as well as working as a grocer. Near that time, Ida's mother came to live with the family in Spokane. She was cared for by Ida until her death some years later.

As happens with memoirs, Pauline's childhood stories gained a distinctly different significance to her in later life than that she might have attributed to them at the time. Many of the reminiscences and reflections represented here were both told to me and were written down at some earlier time, most within the last eight years of her life.[5] Any value in hearing Pauline's life stories lies not solely in one's interest in the childhood stories themselves, but in the synchronic meaning Pauline placed upon those stories many decades later. Pauline began an autobiography at one point that contained some of her reflections. She began with stories of a childhood with parents who lovingly provided her with a space in which to grow. She found it ironic that a child so well cared for to the point of being spoiled was at the same time developing an unspoiled, staunchly independent character. In one early story Pauline introduced the image of the star, an image that would guide her throughout her life and later provide a standpoint from which to make that life meaningful. She reflected upon this possible meaning as she began her story:

> I had thought to begin from here, January 1993, reporting the way in which insights have developed, working backwards to the crib bed of my early childhood, as each new venture into my farther away past developed. But I have finally decided to begin at the beginning and work my way up to the present. I suspect that the record will show how very much my perceptions have deepened with each successive stage. Working backwards, I knew at the start that I would

end in my child's bed, looking up at the stars. But I have decided to begin there, hoping that by the time I have reached the end I will have recapitulated my journey from a meaningful standpoint which was entirely lacking in the doing.

So I begin: Between my brother's birth and mine, mother had adopted the current new policy of letting the child cry until its schedule finally indicated the time to get it up or at least to respond to the crying. Neither of us dreamed how rigid and stubborn and victimized I felt under this regime. But in spite of these strictures and disciplines I grew up happy and secure for my first seven years. I didn't "give anybody any trouble," and one of my early means of making everyone happy was to go to bed voluntarily, without fuss, without help.

I remember—did it happen every night, or do I just remember one night?— kissing mother and father good-night in the kitchen, going upstairs to my dark bedroom, then turning on my light, and undressing and putting on my nightgown, then turning off the light and finding my way to bed, kneeling and saying my prayers: "Now I lay me down to sleep; I pray the Lord my soul to keep. If I should die before I wake, I pray the Lord my soul to take." Then I climbed in and went to sleep. I was properly proud of myself, and my parents were proud of me. No one had come upstairs. No one "helped" in any way. I went to bed, "all alone by myself."

Until this current year of recollecting my past, which I have been systematically doing, I have overlooked what I now consider a prime cause of this exemplary behavior of my childhood. I went to sleep in conscious starlight. My bed lay under a high window, high and wide. My Dad had built this house, and part of the plan was to make the upstairs safe for unattended children. In tracing back the stars of my past this first one suddenly came to me this year. I saw myself as that young child in the dark of my safe room, all alone upstairs, looking out at the stars. I remember one of them as particularly bright; I do wonder now what star it was. ("My Stars! My Journey")

This image of the stars merged, in time, with three other images from Pauline's past, and the story of the "four stars" came to represent her journey. Pauline's story reached far upward into the stars. It was also deeply rooted in the past, as she stretched back in time and into the recesses of her memory for connections, for synchronicity. The same star, we might imagine, followed the wagon train of her ancestors as they trekked across the country. Indeed, Pauline's ancestral heritage was integral to her understanding of herself as a pioneer—of women, of thinkers, of the aged.

ANCESTRY AND CHILDHOOD REFLECTIONS

Pauline's mother, Ida, was born in 1871 to Thomas Paul and Susan Frances Ellis (Zaring) Paul. In the spring of 1862, under the direction of John K.

Kennedy, the Zaring and Paul families were among five families from Iowa that began the trek to Washington Territory over the Oregon Trail. Thomas Paul traveled with his six children and his first wife, Elizabeth, who died on the journey. The trek in covered wagons pulled by oxen took roughly six months, from May to September when the group arrived near Fort Walla Walla, Washington Territory.

Pauline's mother's half sister, Louisa Estes, recalled the journey she made at the age of twelve. She saw a number of Indians along the trail, but surmised the families were never attacked because "we were too well armed and there were too many of us."[6] The John K. Kennedy emigrant train consisted of nearly one hundred covered wagons pulled by oxen. The Kennedy train was to come upon a horrible scene, however, a reminder of the harrowing nature of their journey. As they neared the end of their destination, they learned a wagon train just ahead of them was attacked on August 9, 1862, at American Falls, Idaho, now the site of Massacre Rocks State Park. All but one survivor aboard the train were killed. With a number of men assigned to protect the Kennedy train, they were obliged to camp on nearly the same spot where the massacre took place.

The Paul family finally settled in the Walla Walla valley, meeting Louisa's aunt and uncle, Mary Jane and John McGuire, who had been in the valley for some years. Thomas Paul was a minister in the Methodist Episcopal Church and quickly went to work building a congregation. The *Walla Walla Statesman* indicates he was traveling the area holding revival meetings as early as 1867.[7]

Pauline compiled genealogies and collected numerous photographs and memoirs of her ancestors.[8] She considered her ancestry to be very important, informing her own development as an independent person. She certainly felt her mother clearly came from hearty stock. This realization strengthened Pauline, who later looked to her own childhood for stories of such strength of character. Pauline's later childhood and adolescence included stark realities, illness, abandonment, and relocation; yet, ironically it also contained a great deal of stability. That stability was provided primarily by her mother, the one steady influence in her life throughout the decades. The wisdom and vulnerability of her mother is revealed in the following recollection of Pauline's own emergence as a self-reliant child. On October 14, 1993, Pauline wrote a childhood memory, one which she first remembered recalling in 1961 during a conversation with her Jungian analyst, Renée Brand. Pauline's mother had told her the story in the mid-1940s. "Here is mother's story," Pauline wrote:

> Ma (Grandma) and I were sitting in the dining room. (It had an entry from the kitchen with its outside stairway to the ground, an exit through the living room

and out the front door, and on the opposite wall some five or six feet from us another entry, into the bathroom.)

You and your doll were inseparable. Wherever you went, she was either in your arms or under an arm. You came in from the back yard and went into the bathroom. Almost immediately after the door closed there was a crash and then complete silence. Ma said, in a whisper, "She broke her doll." The silence continued. Ma said, "Ida, go to her." And my mother replied, "I'm afraid to."

Finally, after further silence, you emerged—without your doll—and walked into the living room and across it, headed toward the front door exit.

I couldn't let you go, but I didn't know how to keep you. Your hand was on the doorknob when I said, "Pauline, where is your doll?"

And you replied, in an entirely final voice, "She's gone."

She was never mentioned again.

I went into the bathroom. Her bisque head had apparently crashed against the bathtub. It was completely shattered. Only the staring blue eyes looked up from the bottom of the tub. You had laid out the body on the toilet lid with her clothes neatly arranged, starkly headless.[9]

Pauline discussed many other "learning" experiences from her preteen years, including this particularly poignant memory:

I would not remember that the basement floor was partly dirt except for my devastating experience with my kitten. Two-by-fours had been put on the level dirt and covered with flooring over most, but not all, of the basement; near the stairs, the four-inch space was open at the front. One day my kitten disappeared; we looked and looked in vain. Later in the week, Mother and I went to the basement for something together, and Mother espied and extracted the horrific body of my kitten from that space under the flooring. She had pulled it out by the tail and the effect of the whole body being rigid, standing on the air . . . . As I have said, Dad was doing a lot of building, and I had been impressed with the beauty and sheen of a varnished surface he had created the preceding week. I vaguely remember varnishing my kitten to make him shiny. And I find that now, more than eighty years later, the tears come in the telling. I find I still have no comment. I only know how well I remember my own basement floor as my first place of knowing death. Not only death, but murder. And, moreover, I the murderer. ("Childhood")

Pauline believed her father also provided some stability in her early years. During Pauline's infancy the family was living in Spokane when their house was destroyed by a fire. Her father built them a new house on Thirteenth Avenue in Spokane. The family would move again, however, in 1913 when he got a job as a high school teacher in Colville, Washington. There, they lived in a home that was somewhat rural, yet just three blocks from Pauline's grade school. Her brother, Herbert Melville (also called Rex), was in high school by then. Pauline did not find this move, at age eight, to be disturbing in the least. Pauline recalled,

> I still remember in the fourth or fifth grade writing my address over and over again, with a strong sense of where I belonged in the whole wide world. I would view it with great satisfaction and then write it again. It read, "Pauline Thompson, followed by my now-forgotten address, Colville, Washington; Stevens County; Washington State; United States of America; Western Hemisphere; the World; and finally, the Universe." . . . In all the WORLD I had my own particular place. This was complete stability. This was resilience to change. I was eight and this was my third move. But I was a baby, too young to remember the first move. And my sense of *place* in Colville had been with me, unconsciously, at 917–13th Avenue, and had moved with me to Colville, undisturbed. ("Childhood")

Years later, Pauline would describe Colville as a beautiful, secure place:

> The quiet stars gathered 'round in Colville;
> the world of nature adopted me.
> Nature and books. Not music, for all my lessons. Nor art.
> But nature and books.
> I fed and watched the chickens, shared dad's garden, flowers, insects, even snakes. I grew to love them all,
> So nothing living frightens me, now, I think, except for size. . . .
> It seems, as I look back,
> That I loved beauty,
> And felt it was not mine to have.
> Other people lived in warm and friendly houses and we once did, too,
> But no more.
> My first house was a friendly house. I remember it full of people.
> A birthday party, mine. A big Thanksgiving. A Christmas crowd.
> A club of ladies. Relatives. Neighbors. The ice-cream freezer on the Sunday porch.
> And I belonged. I loved all this and I belonged.
> But I loved Colville more, even without all this, without belonging—
> Because I was older and more aware? or because I met and liked myself? . . .
> [before that] I was Loneliness personified . . .
> [or was it] enforced idleness.[10]

Pauline remembered her father providing the family with routine, such as churning a gallon of ice cream for the family every Sunday in the summer. The cream was saved each week from a cow they had on their country property. She described her assistance in this weekly ritual and her father's parental wisdom when she again asserted herself and found herself in trouble:

> Mother made [the cream mixture] before we left for Sunday school and put it in the ice box. Then when we got home, Mother went to the kitchen to prepare the

customary big Sunday dinner and Dad and I repaired to the basement. We put in the ice cream canister and then while Dad chipped the ice off the cube out of the ice box, I dribbled the salt over it until we got it full and packed it down with gunny sacks and clamped down the handle. Then Dad got out our ice cream plank, a long 2×12. He got the chopping block and put the ice cream freezer up on top of it, centering it between me at one end and the underside of one of the cellar stairs to hold the other in place. This left him free to turn the freezer with both hands. . . .

I once made my role memorable by being very naughty. I had decided that I was being victimized, that I was suffering from a phony occupation, created just to hold me in place. I was being kept out of circulation by a trick. I would find out. Dad had said I was a help, but was he telling the truth? So without warning one Sunday I slid off the end of the plank to see if I made any difference by just sitting there. Salty water, melted ice and, alas, quite a lot of ice cream (the lid came off the canister) mingled on the basement floor in quite a large puddle. . .

.

Only now do I realize how much I should have appreciated my father's reaction. He had red hair and I think still had a lot of the accompanying "ginger," but his reaction was much more powerful than if he had taken any action or even said anything. *Anything.* What he did do was immediately to start mopping up in complete grim silence while I hovered uselessly around him, full of apologies. ("Childhood")

Pauline's memories of her life at eight, nine, and ten in the small Washington town included the wonders of newly introduced technology. She recalled the joy of washday after her father purchased a new washing machine. Instead of scrubbing on a washboard, she could now assist in pushing an "upright stick" back and forth in the new machine. A similar wonder was the wall telephone, at "adult shoulder height, right inside the back door," that her family was to answer when the ring was "three longs and two short." She recalled sitting at the kitchen table while each day her mother shared the neighborhood gossip on the party line. Pauline's memories were more mixed regarding the piano in the living room and her weekly piano lessons: "My teacher [came] once a week and we discussed my very slow control over which fence rails were involved." She remembered her own satisfaction and the pride her father showed, to the extent of waking her up to parade her proudly downstairs and play for guests, after she learned one piece "where I crossed my hands" ("Childhood").

In 1916 Pauline's family returned to Spokane, where Edward landed another job—this time teaching business at Spokane College. Pauline's grandmother moved with them, but died shortly thereafter at the age of eighty. And at age eighteen, her brother Rex left to join the engineering corps serving in World War I. Pauline recalls learning to knit scarves for the war effort, knitting them according to requirements specified by the Red Cross. After the war, Rex made his home in Seattle.[11]

Pauline's father was not to remain to watch Pauline grow up. He was a professor at Spokane University when the war ended, and the family lived in Dishman outside Spokane. He taught until the college folded. Ida was then teaching shorthand at night school. When Edward couldn't find work, they both approached Northwest Business College to see if they could return to work there. The college did not take Edward, but they did employ Ida. Soon after, Edward left for Iowa, vowing when he found work he would send for his family. Ida and the children never heard from him again. At some point, Pauline was aware that her mother hired a detective to find Edward, and he was located in Pawtucket, Rhode Island. Pauline would meet him again when she was thirty years old, but he would never return to his family.[12]

Ida stayed at Northwest Business College until her retirement at age seventy-two. In addition to caring for Pauline, after Pauline's grandmother died, Ida's sister Eva came to live with them in 1917. Eva suffered a stroke in 1918 and required considerable care from Ida for many years. Pauline recalled her twelfth year:

> My twelfth year was unbelievably crowded, hectic, and traumatic. . . . My father left home, ostensibly to find a job in Iowa and send for us. I didn't know he never would; mother did. My totally beloved grandmother, who had lived with us for some years, died. This was not bad enough; she was replaced in our household by an anxiety-depressive aunt. Years later I found that mother was torn all Aunt Eva's life between her terrible conflicting duties toward this older sister and me. Mother told me in my fifties that grandmother, on her deathbed, had asked her to "take care of Aunt Eva."
>
> Mother never discussed her troubles with anyone. Neither did I. Pride saw me through. Saw each of us through. I thought nobody knew how different were my genteel poverty background and my social disgrace (Aunt Eva was a divorcee and this was 1917). Also, of course, the single parent family was an entirely unknown concept, normally never happening unless one parent died. I so envied my friend Gladys; *her* father was safely, decently dead, and everyone was sorry for Gladys.
>
> I know now, *now* I know, that both mother and I might have had perhaps innumerable "support systems," but we didn't know about them, didn't recognize them, and I realize now, spurned some of them unconsciously. ("My Stars! My Journey")

She recalled that after leaving for Colville for Spokane she lost some of that secure, family feeling, and lived without it for many years:

> We left that lovely little quiet town
> Where hospitality dwelt (everywhere except for me)
> And moved away to a place with no grace, no redemption.

A "line of milieu" I hated with all my heart,
And guiltily thought the sin of not adapting was all mine.
"Who am I to criticize?" I felt. "I'm one alien."
"A lonely alien snob." I felt too good for them—
And also less than they for feeling so. (Dreams, 1950, 170)

She was "precocious, always the smartest, always active, always well and strong, always gregarious," and after Colville described herself as a frog in a foreign pond:

The frog and puddle phrase:
I was a big frog—not the biggest—but about the 94th percentile—
That's me, incidentally, in intellect—an A-frog—
But I've never liked my puddle
As did other frogs.
The only trouble, it was the only puddle I knew for many, many years.
(Dreams, 1950, 171)

At age twelve, Pauline did have some good fortune. She met a friend in Latin class she would cherish for most of her life, Erna Bert Nelson. Erna Bert would become a noted Spokane photographer, like each of her siblings, and would photograph Pauline at various times through the coming years.

Pauline entered high school in 1918 at the age of twelve and took her studies very seriously. She graduated from Spokane's North Central High School Classical Course cum laude at the age of sixteen. Pauline then became the first female page in the Spokane public library system. Clearly, part of what saved Pauline from the difficulties of her family life was an opportunity to read when she obtained work in a branch library of some 5,000 volumes. She recalled,

I was soon able to "shelve" very fast, knowing with unerring speed where each book should be put. I had heard about Abraham Lincoln's reading his entire local library in his childhood, and I developed the same ambition. I'm afraid there was a slight difference in purpose and effort; I began on the fiction, which of course predominated. I had read all the children's authors from Alcott and Altsheler (boys' baseball) to Lorhrup's Little Pepper books, which I could not stomach, and on to Zollinger. I had already read in my earlier childhood all the existing Little Colonel stories but when I was twelve, I read *Mary Ware, the Little Colonel's Chum*. This book contains a short story about the star Aldebaran and the Prince Aldebaran.[13]

The story of Aldebaran would provide her images to survive by for the remainder of her life. She recollected,

Aldebaran is "the red eye of Taurus," God of War. I met this star in a child's short story when I gravely needed it; I was facing major crises at ages eleven and twelve. The story is about Aldebaran the man, a Prince whose stars foretold the unmatched courage and prowess with which he would wield "the Sword of Conquest." Because he was born in Mars' month the bloodstone became his signet, sure token that undaunted courage would be the jewel of his soul.[14]

However, injured early in his promised hero's life of victory and conquest, Aldaberan lived out his life, instead, as a town jester. Pauline noted this was not only different from the prophecies, but represented an opposite fate from that which was prophesied. As a jester, Aldebaran "swore by the bloodstone on his finger that he would keep his oath till the going down of one more sun," his oath being each day to live his shattered life, one day at a time, as a crippled clown instead of the greatest Prince of them all. He was finally able to formulate his new life by reformulating the prophecy. Pauline continued, "As Aldebaran the star shines in the heavens, no light within itself, but borrowed from the Central Sun, so shall Aldebaran the man shine among his fellows, beggared of joy himself but gathering happiness from door to door as beggars gather crusts" ("Four Stars").

Pauline wore a ring with a red stone given to her by her Aunt Eva on her "marriage" finger most of her life. She saw the ring stone as symbolizing "*Aldebaran*, the Red Eye of Taurus, sure token that undaunted courage would be the jewel of (my) soul." During her traumatic twelfth year of life, Pauline said, "I had constant recourse to my star and my ring. I needed both of them most of the time" ("Four Stars").

EARLY IMAGES OF THE FOUR STARS

Pauline was beginning to dream of her future, determined, among other things, to become a medical doctor. She would not attain this dream, nor would her periodic romantic notions of intimacy become reality. More often, she would make a "fool" out of herself, becoming involved in what she saw in retrospect as unsuitable relationships. "I'm looking back now" Pauline wrote in 1993,

. . . to the contents of this inner story and I wonder how much was my fate and how much did I deliberately choose—*make*—my fate when I, like Aldebaran, started out to surpass everyone in heroism only to become finally the crippled town jester. Aldebaran was a very tough, complex guy; I still am interested in him. ("Four Stars")

Pauline may have seen her father as the fool, having left the family. His leaving would affect Pauline for many years, contributing to her difficulty in forming intimate relationships. Once he left, the routine he provided was gone; never again would she experience such stability in life.

Pauline wrote of an experience at age sixteen in which she again saw herself "reflected" in a particular star. Her own life, she saw, was a reflection of a greater star. She told this story:

> Four years later I had an interesting experience when my mother took me to visit relatives in Seattle. I was sixteen so my first cousin Muriel must have been twenty-one. The three of us went out to Uncle Henry's farm for an afternoon of meeting Uncle Henry and Aunt Rachel. . . . Uncle Henry had just recently painted the sides of his well above the water line with creosote and then the rainy season had brought the water back up over the line. . . . I can now envision myself, can recall my lying on my stomach on the well curb, looking down the well. The water, of course, looked coal black, being some 25 or 30 feet down, probably. The amazing thing was that reflected in the well was a star. I went in to ask mother about it. And mother explained that the stars were always alight, that we didn't know it because of the closer daylight. When you shut out the importunate foreground, even though you couldn't see the star in the sky, it was reflected in the bottom of the well. Star above; same star below. ("My Stars! My Journey")

Pauline recalled that she thought no more about the stars at the time. However, when she began Jungian analysis in 1952, she painted a series of "active imagination" paintings in which the star again appeared. She painted not just a star, but the star above and in the bottom of the well. Even then, when she reflected upon the paintings, Pauline did not attach a great deal of importance to the stars. It was not until forty years later, in 1992, that she happened upon those paintings in the course of writing up her memoirs.

The emergence of images of stars at crucial points in her life became proof to Pauline that her life carried a theme, and that this theme was profoundly meaningful. The star in the bottom of the well was a reflection of the star above that cannot always be seen. Pauline saw her life and herself as reflecting the spirit world, the world where life has more meaning than, say, common experiences she lived as a school girl, like being humiliated when wearing a completely inappropriately crinkled dress, or cutting her hair and realizing it made one look simply like a "hedgehog" ("Childhood"). The star was a reflection of a world where what was important was the overall, the unity one was unable to perceive in the midst of living and even in the immediate reflection, as we shall see in the chapters ahead, over which job to take at a given moment with its accompanying subsequent regrets, or which person with whom to consummate an intimate relationship followed by its inevitable trail of grief.[15]

Throughout her life, Pauline would fret over individual decisions regarding career and relationships. Yet, by 1992, Pauline came to see not just the story she was putting together, but herself, as a reflection of a life that was greater than the materiality or the decisiveness of the moment. She would come to see herself as on a "soul journey" from the moment she first peered out that child's bedroom window and gazed upon a star. In 1993, Pauline wrote about why she saw the paintings of the stars as "such a profound shock." She came to understand the image of herself "lying on the curb, looking up, looking down" as representing "I the see-er, I the seer." She continued:

> Seeing a unity, seeing the totality of the spirit world; seeing how it contains the incarnated world, seeing simultaneously the reality of the encompassing spirit world by *reflection*. . . . In 1992 I had the very rare privilege of ending this life's journey in the course of embarking on a new journey. I have told you all the preliminary steps of which I am aware. There may be others, of course; I didn't know these [four stars] until they cropped up in my retrospecting. The whole point . . . is that there was the star *all my life* expanding and particularizing and becoming more and more personal as the years went by. . . . And all unconscious in their time. Of course, one can change the past. In fact, one can't *not* change the past if one's way of looking has developed at all. ("My Stars! My Journey")

Eventually Pauline imaged four stars. The first main star was Aldebaran, the red eye of Taurus, God of War.[16] The second main star was the Star of Bethlehem, the star's light she ceased to follow when she left the church between the ages of nineteen and forty-nine ("Four Stars"). The third star was represented by the star Pauline saw when she looked into her Uncle Henry's well at the age of twelve, then discovered in a painting she composed at age forty-seven, and recalled again at eighty-seven. The star at the bottom of the well, possibly a reflection of a star that had already died, could not be seen except "in the darkness at the well-bottom" where its reflection became visible. The star at the bottom signified, for Pauline, her own unconscious. Finally, the fourth star represented herself, the "seer" at the well curb. As seer, she could block out the light of the star at the bottom, just as she could block out the unconscious ("Four Stars").

For Pauline, the images of two main and two lesser stars came to represent the personal and archetypal unconscious, both containing darkness and light. She wrote:

> *As I see it*, my currently uppermost image of four particular stars has given me that place to stand whereon some scientist said, "If I had a lever and a place to

stand I could move the world." I feel an obligation to share my experience of as-
suredness of a place to stand. The world has had to put up with me off-balance
and askew for almost nine decades! Let me now testify that doors still open and
new lights shine, apparently right up to the last gasp, and I more firmly and se-
curely "stand on my own two feet" than I ever have before. . . . The power in
my four stars lies in their rightness for me; they circumscribe *my* place to stand.
I can bring forth what is in me better for being framed within these four stars. I
feel safely enclosed, as if in a Christian painting with the four evangelists, one
in each corner. ("Four Stars")

Pauline's "spiritual" journey would begin and continue as if "safely enclosed . . . in a Christian painting." During her middle years she would ac-
complish professionally more than the vast majority of twentieth-century
women, including women today. She would leave a remarkable legacy
as teacher, nurse, psychologist, and friend. But her notion of living "safely
enclosed" would not be a constant: the many middle years of her life would
be characterized by personal turmoil and questionable decisions, as we shall
see in the next chapters.

A BLIND DATE

Pauline entered college as a premed student at Washington State College in
Pullman in 1921.[17] One final adolescent memory from her college years cap-
tures Pauline's unique intensity as she emerged from these early years in eastern Washington. She was a practical person, yet one who, even though she
tried, could not experience life frivolously without engaging in analysis or
theological or philosophical musings. Pauline still considered herself a Christian when she entered college, although her notions of Christianity were already becoming metaphorical in that she would not accept any literal or
straight forward interpretations of traditional religion. In the following mem-
oir, we witness a person one could either run from or be mesmerized by in her
search for meaning. This telling of Pauline's behavior on a date is comical, although I suspect her date was not himself amused as he discovered the complexity of this woman, until now a stranger to him:

I remember a blind date I had in my last year of college. My friend and her
boyfriend took me and my date up to Round Top, where they produced two
blankets and we separated a suitable distance for the business of the evening. I
was determined at this point to behave like other women so I went along with
the gag, pardon the pun, as long as it stayed above the waistline. Then I balked.

After a certain amount of invective from my frustrated companion, *we* talked. He proved to be an interesting conversationalist, particularly when we got around to discussing the merits of the virgin birth. I put forward my case that He [Jesus] either was or He wasn't the product of such a union and that the correct answer was of unsurmountable importance. In retrospect, I can see why the frustrated young man was not impressed with his evening. He made one more attempt to change me from my orthodox ways, offering to take me to a movie and driving out into the countryside instead.

He soon found himself saying, "Well, if that's the way you want to act, you'll sure die an old maid." And I said, with equal fury, "I'd rather die an old maid than to live the way you do."[18]

Pauline reflected upon her childhood as a time when she lay under a transcendent star that encompassed her, keeping her safe throughout those years. She saw this metaphorically as star of Bethlehem, a star that came to rest over the place where the child Jesus, and later the child Pauline, lay. She would follow another image of the star—that of the fool—into relationships and missed opportunities as she moved into adolescence and young adulthood.

Chapter Two

Professional Training, Work, and Relationships

Does it require deep intuition to comprehend that man's ideas, views, and conceptions, in one word, man's consciousness, changes with every change in the conditions of his material existence, in his social relations and in his social life?

Karl Marx, *The Communist Manifesto*

It's not very sensible to deny realities. The recourse when they get too grim and/or overwhelming is to focus, really focus, a little attention on other aspects of our life that are not grim or overwhelming. If pleasure won't stab us awake, we can woo it; we don't have to pray that God will stab us with pain instead; we can induce our own wakefulness. I am a more than normally sentient person, I think. (I enjoy so much that does not give pleasure to most.) It is my duty, as well as my right, to be aware of pleasure and beauty and rapture—to dance with joy. Only so can I bear to come to grips with pain and suffering as I should.

Pauline Thompson, "To Accept Pain"

Pauline knew from a young age that she wanted to be a doctor. From an early age into her first year of college she was convinced she had been "called" by God to do so. She was profoundly religious and talked about her vocational call:

I believed with all my faith that I had been "called" by God; I had a special vocation—"vocatus": *called* by God to fulfill a specific lifework in His behalf. I was to be a doctor, and I do not mean Doctor of Education, which I eventually became; I didn't know there was such a career and I would have scorned it if I had. I was called to be a *doctor*-doctor, meaning that I wanted to become a

19

doctor, called as Samuel was called in "Here am I, Samuel." I was called to make sick people well. I have never known why I had this compulsion. There were no doctors—ever—in either my father's or my mother's families, so far as I know, not even among mother's myriads of relatives. Nor do I know when this message came to me; I do know that out of my weekly allowance of ten cents a week, from ages eight to ten, I sent $5.00 a year to my bank account in Spokane to go into my college fund to be a doctor. . . . [Later] I added a factor: I would become a missionary doctor serving in China. I wonder why China; what did I read or hear? (Oh, I think our missionary barrels went there at that time.) I didn't mind that I could not marry, that I had to get all A's if I could, that I would have to sacrifice and self-deny and scrimp. The more handicaps the more to the Glory of God that I would fulfill His divine will. Selah.[1]

A VOCATIONAL BLOW

Pauline's strong sense of vocation was crushed, however, when she was informed, perhaps ironically by a physician, that she was not strong enough to undergo the rigors of medical training. Pauline wrote:

When I returned to college for my sophomore year, I enrolled in organic chemistry, college algebra, German (I had already planned to finish, if possible, at the Johns Hopkins University and do post-doctoral study at the University at Leipzig), biology, and I forget what else—a tight schedule fitted around fifteen hours a week working in the college library. I lasted two weeks. A routine physical checkup on all the girls in the college disclosed a heart murmur, an appallingly high blood pressure, and urine specimens solid with albumin. The school physician had me immediately taken out of school and sent home, after which she became my personal physician—she and I were both from Spokane, and mother and I had never had a physician before. I later learned that she told mother that I might be dead in six months. Instead, I recovered, and when spring semester loomed Dr. Houston told me: "You can go back to school and even take lab courses or you can work, but you will never be able to do both again." ("Bertha Myself")

The coming years would all hinge upon this physician's one proclamation. Pauline was crushed. She wrote:

My sense of direction, of meaning, of purpose, of goal became disoriented as I continued to absorb into myself those two simple clauses: "you can take lab courses. Or you can work." Three years before, when I was graduated from high school's Classical Course at sixteen, with honors, I had met with another bitter alternative. I had been accepted at Leland Stanford as a pre-med student when

Stanford was only beginning to accept women students at all; now the charter limit was 500, and I was to be one of them. But when I returned my entrance form, I asked about employment in the college library. And the reply was: "We do not allow our pre-medical students to work during the school year. The curriculum is too demanding." I had survived this blow by foregoing Stanford and entering the nearest "cow college" instead. Also I worked, full-time, for two years before I entered. I had been pitifully proud of having completed high school at age sixteen. However, I comforted myself that, though I had lost those two years, I was still not "behind."

Now I had to face an entire adaptation to a totally different future, not just to my immediate future. ("Bertha Myself")

Pauline accepted her doctor's words as final. She was being prevented from medical school not, apparently, because of her gender or ability, but because of her health and because of her class, and the fact that her social standing and economic situation would not enable her the luxury of studying without also working.

Not only was Pauline vocationally off course, she was thrown into a spiritual crisis that would be sustained throughout the next thirty years. God had called her to be a doctor, she knew. Now where was God? Pauline wrote:

"You can go back to school and even take lab courses or you can work, but you will never be able to do both again."

That was the sentence that changed my life.

It is unfortunate that I have the temperament I have; nobody, not even mother, knew that this sentence was a death sentence. It became all in an instant the basis of the major neurosis of most of my life. My "calling" went. And with it went my belief in God. I was becoming very rationalist in those days, logical, reductive. I worked my spiritual life down to this: Either there wasn't any God and I have been praying to the ceiling all those childish years; or, conceivably, there was a God but not for me. I had thought we were in touch, but obviously we weren't. ("Bertha Myself")

Her choice of vocation would shift numerous times over the coming years. Indeed, the loss of faith that accompanied her grudging yet complete acceptance of the news that she could not be a doctor would rob Pauline of her single-minded pursuit of a vocational vision.

Many years later, Pauline would still feel the pain of her unfulfilled career and life goal. At the age of forty-six, she wrote the following poem for her Jungian analyst, Renée Brand, whom she loved and respected dearly. In the poem, she infers that Renée recognized Pauline would have made a good physician, by saying she would not have had "a bad hand" at it.

Not a Bad Hand for a Physician
Renée.
To be a physician.
That is what I want.
That's what I really want.
It will not be put down.
Dr. Thompson, pediatrician;
Clinic director, school doctor,
Lecturer, med. school teacher,
Maybe child psychiatrist—
None of the later specialties would be difficult to build—
To choose and build—
As they are now—If I were M.D. now.
I would not be lost.

"Not a bad hand for a physician," she said,
"Not a bad hand at all.". . .

In longing tears.
That's what I want.
All this other; all has been expediency and substitute. . . .
Some school would take me now, Renée.
I'm sure *some* school would take me now.

"Not a bad hand for a physician."
Oh, Renée, my heart cries out as it did at 19,
But now at last I heed. Is it too late?
No sacrifice of mine would be too great.
Renée, I would even leave you,
Tonight; I could come back to you,
But this is unfinished business
From all my life.
I thought from childhood that I was born for this.
Where now I say "the Way."[2]

Between 1925 and 1926, as a result of this absolute blow to her vocational identity, Pauline shifted her focus from medicine to teaching. She turned her pursuits toward an elementary school teaching diploma at Cheney State Normal School (now Eastern Washington University) and received a special normal school diploma. She then continued her study at Washington State College, earning a B.A. in Education and a five-year normal school diploma, cum laude, in 1927. She went on to earn a master's degree in English in 1928.

Pauline's college years were both academically and socially successful. She was elected to the professional English fraternity Sigma Tau Delta, the Honor Society Phi Kappa, as well as to Pi Lambda Theta at Washington State

College. She was awarded a teaching appointment to teach college freshman English as a master's student at Washington State College. During those years Pauline developed friendships that would continue throughout her life. She and Erna Bert Nelson knew one another at North Central High School in Spokane and became closer friends as sorority sisters in Sigma Kappa Sorority. Margaret Truesdale and Pauline also forged a friendship that would grow throughout the years.[3] Upon her graduation from WSC, Pauline taught English at Pullman High School from 1928 to 1930. There, she met another person who would become a close friend. Hal Richardson was a fifteen-year-old sophomore when Pauline began teaching at the age of twenty-three. She recalled that Hal approached her in the hallway on the first day of school. She wrote, "I think I felt the force of his great talent, and I like to imagine that I was instantly aware of the friendship that was to come."[4] Hal became a successful writer and corresponded with Pauline for many years.

PROFESSIONAL SHIFTS AND COMMUNIST LEANINGS

Pauline's restlessness with her career emerged early on. She would return to school for further and different qualifications more than once more. Not content to stay in Washington as a high school teacher, Pauline determined to advance her own education and enrolled in Teachers College at Columbia University in New York City. There, she seems to have managed both studies and work. For, in addition to her course work, she worked as a personal secretary to Harold Rugg, an accomplished professor of education at Teachers College. At the end of 1933, Pauline earned a master's degree in curriculum. That same year she received a fellowship to study the history of education.

During her years at Teachers College, Pauline developed socialist leanings. Many at Teachers College emerged from the Depression years with the belief that education was integral to social progress.[5]

Pauline found herself disgusted with government programs and rhetoric that claimed to put people back to work but fell, in her view, far short of what was needed. She wrote of her views in a letter to a friend, dated September 15, 1933:

> I'm having a grand time writing radical pamphlets (I needn't sound so plural, only two of them) and having the powers-that-be take all the pep out of them. They are about *Public Works and Re-employment* and include resumes of the Wagner-Lewis bill—? million relief to states; Wagner bill—establishing National Employment Service Bureaus; C.C.C.—Roosevelt's pretty idea of young men reforesting; the $3 billion 300 million public works and the Muscle Shoals and Tennessee Valley Act. I'm so full of legislation and government and disgust

at profit and sorrow for the 18 million unemployed and rage at the middlemen, etc. etc. that I run out the ears with it. Fortunately I must be through [with school] by the first of October, so Jean [my roommate] will have a bit of peace then. How I am prone to come and shout before I get in the door, "Hey, did you know that only 200 people are getting employed on the Muscle Shoals dam and the papers say a million?"[6]

In 1934, Pauline published a small booklet entitled *Uncle Sam and Unemployment*. The book was referred to in a *New York Post* review as the "first textbook on unemployment," and by Teachers College Dean William F. Russell as one in a series of texts on the "New Deal." Russell continued, "It has been our aim to produce a fair and unbiased statement of the problem and an impartial analysis of the solutions proposed."[7] A *New York Post* review described *Uncle Sam and Unemployment* this way:

> The causes and effects of the depression are unfolded in story book form in the first text book for grammar school children on unemployment.
>   It is called, "Uncle Sam and Unemployment" and is published today by Teachers College, Columbia University. Six members of the faculty, under the direction of Dr. Pauline E. Thompson, collaborated in writing the book.
>   The text book tells the story of the Prestons, a typical American family. It describes how they were affected by the stock market crash of 1929, how Preston lost his job, how the family adjusted itself to poverty, and, finally, how it was forced to seek relief.[8]

The book offered the message that although workers had been able to help themselves in the past, such was no longer the case. Government assistance was essential: Americans believed that any one who wasn't too lazy to work could find a job. The story of the Prestons illustrated one case in which conditions over which the family had no control forced them, like many other families, into unemployment.

Pauline quietly joined efforts of the Communist party, so strong was her belief that the government, as the government of the people, needed to take responsibility for the millions who were unemployed.[9]

RELATIONSHIPS AND ABORTION

Pauline's study of poverty and the depression led her to understand that women were clearly financially better off as married women than as single. Later she would articulate this view in a letter to a friend. She agreed with her friend that "one recoils instinctively" to one scholar's idea that women should not marry. She wrote:

Unmarried schoolteachers are neurotic almost by definition. New York City is so full of them (to keep it strictly impersonal!) that one of the questions on our physical exam is whether or not we have ever sought the services of a psychiatrist. (While there is possibly no connection sought by the question, there is a connection found in the answers.)

My own conclusion is that the only differences that exist between the sexes are 1. biological and 2. social. And on both counts, women would be better off married than men. . . .[10]

The letter continued with an explanation of two further points: first, those women who want "a greater measure of freedom" should not marry, for "promiscuous marriages" are worse than not marrying. Secondly, however, women will achieve a "better standard of living" if married.

Given her views, it comes as no surprise that Pauline met a man she hoped to marry. She met Wilbur Gooch in 1930 at the age of twenty-five and became involved with him for the next three years. The only stumbling block in her passionate wish that Wilbur would agree to marry her was the fact that Wilbur was already a married man.

Pauline wrote a sort of contract, or marriage proposal, to Wilbur, offering him a room in the house she shared with her longtime friend Jean. In it, she illustrated both her fierce independence and her wish for "great happiness" in an equal, "amiable" partnership. She listed hours she and Jean were away and would not bother him, and she promised the following:

No one will ever come into your room except by urgent invitation.
You are welcome to all the house privileges you want.
The only stipulation is that you marry me before moving in.
I do not want your name, your time, or your money.
If you want to leave at any time for any cause or no cause, you may. . . .
I want you to do this. . . .
if giving great happiness instead of great misery would please you—
think upon it. (Correspondence, 12 September 1933)

In her relationship with Wilbur, Pauline was sexually active for the first time in her life. When she became pregnant during her affair Pauline went to a doctor who felt her health was not strong enough for Pauline to carry a baby and agreed to perform a therapeutic abortion. Pauline wrote in her diary that she "rationalized at the time that we would conceive him again as soon as we were married."[11]

Pauline kept a diary chronicling her love affair and abortion experience from February 4 through November 28, 1931. Her daily entries include recordings of mundane occurrences such as whether she slept in a given morning, had a good breakfast or washed her silks, as well as countless hours spent preparing curriculum, meeting with students, and grading papers. She also wrote of many hours spent with Wilbur, whom she described as "all of everything that's good, lovely, funny, appreciative—everything—and all in reason."[12] On the day she wrote those words, she went into the hospital, where for several days she felt deliriously comfortable and cared for.

A manuscript entitled "Abortion," written in 1991, reveals that in spite of her apparent naïveté in 1931 at being cared for by Wilbur and blindly in love, Pauline was aware of her inner self enough to know the decision to abort was, and would always be, the right decision for her. Her 1931 diary reveals she did have a sense of her own identity as it was affected by this experience. After her surgery, she noted, "Slept for the first time in months like my old self. Woke up and dreamt and all, but I had again that elusive feeling of identity" ("Diary Fragment"). Pauline began her 1934 work entitled "Abortion" this way, after she had a second abortion:

> I think my two abortions were the most traumatic events of my entire life. They are my deepest grief, deeper than my last hopeless adult love. They were my deepest grief at the time they occurred. In other landmark events of my life I feel that my fate was thrust upon me, but my abortions were solely my choice, my responsibility, my voluntary sacrifices. I was not helplessly forced to have them, as so many are; I was not even coerced. I actively, consciously, caused both of these dreadful events. As I watched myself going through each of them I viewed myself with horror. I still do.
>
> But in like circumstances, I would repeat them both.[13]

Pauline argued in her paper that abortion can never be anyone's choice but an individual woman's. She carefully drew arguments regarding the sacredness of life beginning at birth ("When you pick up a chestnut, are you holding a live chestnut tree? How old was Adam when God created him? . . ." ["Abortion" 12]); horrible experiences of unwanted babies born she witnessed as a nurse on maternity wards; the certainty that none of us has Godlike knowledge (not only can another not judge her for her right to abort, but she cannot judge another who chooses to fulfill all pregnancies); the absurdity of our willingness to legalize killing on the battlefield or electric chair, then to call abortion "murder;" and the expulsion of men from abortion decisions: "there exists intractable and irreversible fundamental male-female inequality. . . . I was *compelled* to make the choice . . . men have no such compulsion" ("Abortion" 26).

But Pauline's most innovative argument in her recitative for a woman's "right to choose" was from the point of view not of women's rights, but of the child's. She argued that a fetus should have the right *not* to be born. It is not always the best thing for a child to come into the world in particularly difficult circumstances: "As it now stands . . . a fetus does NOT have the right to life. It has a *compulsion* to life, an entirely different matter. If the fetus has a right not to live, then choice is involved" ("Abortion" 24).

Pauline argued further that sometimes a fetus must wait until later to join a mother in a family with a life together worth living. She wrote:

> I had said in March to Junior, "Sorry, darling, but you'll have to wait. You have jumped the gun. If you were to come now, I would have to commit suicide. Well, that doesn't make sense—you *can't* come now, no matter what, because, if I committed suicide before your birth, there wouldn't be any birth anyway. . . . You cannot *be*, and so you cannot ever become. Not now. Next year you will be a fulfillment, will grace all three of our lives, all of our lives long. Goodbye for now. Just wait a while. I'm sorry. I love you. . . ."
>
> So I had an abortion. At Presbyterian Hospital, all Park-Avenue legal and above board. Legally: "continued pregnancy would endanger your life." The operation *had* actually become "therapeutic" by the time I had it, though I was in perfect health on 16th January. I had visits from my supposed husband-would-never-be-father, and my nurses commiserated with us that this tragedy had befallen such a "lovely, lovely, loving couple." I forget what name I used. I had no other visitors. I told my close friend Helen, who lived in the same dormitory as I, that I was having a hemorrhoidectomy and that I wasn't going to tell her which hospital because I knew how busy she was, and I didn't want visitors anyway because I would be home so soon. I was in the hospital two days. . . .
>
> Physically, it was nothing. Psychologically, there was no erasure. They say, "time heals all wounds." How much time? I'm obviously not going to have enough time. That was Easter of 1931 and now in 1991, I look back and the regret is not faded nor has the thwarted love and the pain ceased to stab. Sixty years! Some scars time does not heal.
>
> Two years later I found out beyond denial that my supposed future husband was still living with his wife on weekends, across the river, in a another state. . . .
>
> I had not waited, sexually, till marriage. Several of my friends had not waited, either, but they were much luckier than I. Not only did they get their men, but they did not consider that they had sinned in the process. I sinned because I thought I did and, sinner, felt I deserved what I got. I do not say that my friends sinned in doing the very same thing I did, because I do not know what they thought and could not "really" know, and it was none of my business anyway. But *I* had sinned. I loved Tom [Wilbur],[14] and I didn't wait for our marriage, so when Junior came bursting in, he had to wait for our marriage too. As it turned out, we both have had to wait—forever—Junior and I. ("Abortion" 29–32)

Pauline reflected upon this "waiting" and its rightness, in spite of its pain. And she expanded upon an additional reasons why one should not judge another for abortion—that not only does a child not always have a right to be born, but a woman does not always have a right to bring another into the world:

> The "right-to-life" people will tell you that Junior at least had a right to become. I don't think he had any more "rights" than the other six [I hoped someday to have]. They were all central to my inner life, my potential life, but my potential way of life shall we say "miscarried," and Junior's potential way of life shall we say "miscarried" too, and his potential birth aborted along with all the rest. I found that I had no right to the life I foresaw the night of his conception. . . . I submit that all seven had a theoretical right to life, though especially and particularly, of course, Junior. And I know—I know, and I am me, none other—I know that they had a greater right not to be. ("Abortion" 30–33)

Pauline wrote positively of her affair with Wilbur through November 1931, when she began to learn the "truth" that he would not leave his wife. Later, when it finally became clear that Wilbur had no intention of leaving his wife for Pauline, she "put him out," tired of the "lies" and of "living in sin."[15]

After breaking up her relationship with Wilbur, Pauline had a visit from her mother, with whom she seems to have enjoyed a close and loving relationship throughout her life. Pauline wrote to her friend Erna Bert Nelson in 1933,

> Mother and I had a swell time when she was here. . . . Mother made the trip for $74. . . .
>
> The depression got me finally; my love's young dream with Wilbur is gradually faded. Mother came more to see if I would survive and how things were than anything else, I think. Unfortunately Wilbur was out of town at a convention that week so she didn't see him; but she found me so fat and frisky that it doesn't matter. I am to work six days a week, and he is working six nights a week, and neither of us have any money, so I imagine that is that. (Correspondence, 1933)

With "that being that," and her relationship with Wilbur over, Pauline was pleased to settle down with her roommate, Jean. In May and June, between the end of the school year at Teachers College and the start of work as secretary to Dr. Harold Rugg, Jean and Pauline took a three-week bicycle trip to Marble Head Neck, Massachusetts. A diary, written jointly by the two friends, chronicles their trip and stay at a cabin on the sea. Pauline wrote as a forward to the diary: "Jean was as near to being a sister as any relationship I've ever had. We were together 24 hours a day and 7 days a week for more than a year and remained friends until Jean's death in 1962."[16] By September, the two had settled into a rhythm as roommates. Pauline wrote Erna Bert, ". . . as Jean has told you, she and I are going domestic, and I'm pleased as punch. The apartment looks good to me, after all my years of rattling around and Jeannie is a swell person to live with, as you probably suspect" (Correspondence, 1933).

PROFESSIONAL AND MARITAL EMBARRASSMENT

In spite of Pauline's penchant for nontraditional relationships, her affair with Wilbur being the first of a series, she continued to hold quite traditional values regarding marriage itself. She believed a man and a woman should not "live in sin," as she put it, meaning being engaged in a sexual relationship outside of marriage. Perhaps it was the strength of that belief that caused her to move quickly to get married when she fell in love again.

In the fall of 1933, Pauline met Lloyd Victory, a printer. After a four-month courtship, the two were married on the ninth of February in 1934. Victory did not have a job at the time as the printing trade was saturated with qualified workers. He went to the unemployment office each morning to see if he could secure work, even for a limited amount of time. Pauline, upon graduating from Teachers College, was offered a position teaching in a prestigious private school in Akron, Ohio. She claimed the couple felt they had no choice but to take the offer for a job and salary, and she and Victory moved to Akron, where she taught English and served as dramatic coach at the Old Trail School. Pauline would have preferred to use her maiden name professionally, but she was forced to become "Mrs. Victory" at the conservative private school.

At the Old Trail School, Pauline worked with rather well-to-do high school students, whom she came to enjoy. She worked many hours a week, especially when coaching an upcoming drama production. Lloyd, being unemployed but having some carpentry skills, at times accompanied her to work on putting up the sets for productions.

Pauline quietly joined the efforts of the Communist party in Akron. She explained: "I was a WASP Republican by birth, training, and predilection. Immediately on being introduced to communism, I converted. 'From each according to his ability; to each according to his need.' Simplicity of course, it wasn't easy because this tenet is obviously quite impossible in a WASP world."[17] When, however, the party members wanted her to hand out leaflets, she realized she could not be seen publicly supporting them for fear of losing her job. She later recalled:

> I secretly joined the Communist Party. I secretly attended meetings and took courses and fulminated helplessly at the political disorder I witnessed, but I had learned well that making a noise about it was a good way to join the breadlines. . . .

> I had gone [to Akron, Ohio] to teach in a private school, and had located and joined a Communist unit there the first week I arrived. The idiots in charge assigned me the duty of handing out leaflets on the streets of central Akron. I never went back.[18]

It turned out not to be her political affiliations, but the fact that Pauline as well as Lloyd devoted extra hours to the school, that would cost Pauline her teaching job at Old Trail School. Mr. Hinton, the school administrator, sent her a letter of review in November of 1934. In her seven-page reply, she commented upon his one favorable and four adverse comments on her work at Old Trail School. The latter included Pauline's appearance, the inappropriate neighborhood in which she resided, and the fact that she was married to Mr. Victory.

Pauline responded by noting that her economic situation prevented her from focusing time or money on her appearance: it was difficult to buy clothing on a budget of fifty-three cents a day. Regarding being "married to Mr. Victory," Pauline admitted he had "intended to remain divorced from all contacts with any position I might ever be in professionally," and that he would certainly do so from now on. However, Pauline was responsible, as part of her job as an English teacher, to direct drama productions and found herself working constantly with few breaks and little help. She wrote: "I do not know what comment arose when he jumped into the breach the night of the play; I do not much care. I needed him extremely. He, Miss Shepherd, and I were the only ones even faintly competent to carry on the unexpected duty of lighting. . . ."[19] Pauline admitted her husband was a rather unkempt person, and if he was an embarrassment to her, he must have truly appalled the school's sense of appropriate appearance for those in contact with students.

Again, Pauline explained that it was due to economic circumstances that she and Lloyd chose the unfortunate location of their residence. As Lloyd was unable to find steady work (discouraged, many mornings he did not even attempt the journey to the unemployment office), the couple was forced to rent an apartment in a less expensive district some distance from Old Trail School. Pauline acceded in her letter to Hinton:

> No one but a fool would think that we like living where we are . . . .
> I must tell you, however, that there is nothing indecent or undercover that I can discover in our location. It is in a noisy district, and a dirty one; and it borders on the Negro section. It quite possibly *has* been a house of ill-fame in the past . . . .

What Pauline did not know was just *how* embarrassing it was to the school to have one of their teachers residing there. She discovered the building was indeed used for prostitution (possibly even when she and Lloyd lived there)—and further, it seemed the building was owned by a member of the Board of Trustees of Old Trail School.

Pauline received a notice of termination from the president of Old Trail School at the end of her first year. She appealed the decision, promising to make "the adjustment necessary" in her personal life. Recognizing that "your appeal has strengthened your position with us," Mr. Hinton reaffirmed her termination but promised to give favorable references for future employment.[20] Pauline's year in Akron, as it turned out, had all these and more elements of a tragic comedy. Though her marriage was happy at the start, that happiness waned as Lloyd became more and more complacent about both his appearance and getting a job. Interestingly, the play Pauline directed that not only exhausted her but also was a catalyst for her firing from Old Trail School was about complex problems within a family.[21] The *Akron Times-Press* described the play this way:

> Every family has its problems. But never in anyone's wildest imagination could there be any more complicated worries than those of the Hardy family, which seniors at Old Trial School are showing in their play, "Skidding.". . . Mrs. L. L. Victory, dramatic instructor, is director.
>
> It may be the modern age. The audience will draw its own conclusion after the final curtain bow. Not only is Marion, Miss Norma Post who plays the lead, torn between love and politics, but her two married sisters leave their husbands and come home to live. Her father loses his election for judge and her mother leaves home. Can more complications be imagined?[22]

Indeed, more complications not only could be imagined, but were occurring in Pauline's personal life in this "modern age." For if troubles with her school administration were not enough, Pauline soon had two more terrible personal revelations as she settled in Akron. She discovered that Lloyd was in fact already married when she and he "married." Not only had she been "living in sin" with Wilbur some years before, she was living in a bigamous relationship with Lloyd. And second, she discovered she was pregnant. Years later, she would reflect:

> I married Dick [Lloyd] although he had told me he was sterile. I would have to forego motherhood. The depression was on; Dick was unemployed; my boss [at Teachers College] had gone to Liberia, leaving me unemployed; and married women at that time were not allowed to teach in the public schools. So the one blessing was that at least Dick knew, knew, that he was sterile. I couldn't—we couldn't—have a baby, anyway.

But he wasn't. I had the second abortion when I found out accidentally that he, too, had a living wife—with whom, oddly enough, he had truly fallen out of touch ten years previously! Second time; same song; almost the same verse; same place, same timing, different name. The second abortion was even more "therapeutic" than the first.

"Why didn't you tell me about her?" I asked. "Because," he said, "I knew you wouldn't wait for me." I had no response to that; I knew it was true. ("Abortion" 35–36)

Pauline knew some institutions would not employ a married woman, let alone a mother, as a teacher. She mused about whether her decision to abort was based upon some knowledge at the time that her marriage would not last, then wrote, ". . . anyway, I *had* to work" ("Personal Events"). She sought out the physician who had performed her earlier abortion, who agreed "with much more truth than before" that her life would be endangered if she persisted in carrying to term a pregnancy. "'Perhaps under other circumstances,' he said. . . . And given circumstances led me to formulate my own ethical and moral code, which read: don't bear this child, either" ("Abortion" 36).

Pauline did not confront and kick Lloyd out immediately upon learning that he was already married. Her own sense of self instead caused her to believe that perhaps this deception was what she deserved both for having had abortions and for living in sin.

Pauline wrote of her relationship with Wilbur and of marrying Lloyd on the rebound from the former relationship:

We [Wilbur and I] were both working on our doctorates; I helped him with his; he got it. I got mine three matriculations and seventeen years later. . . . I married Lloyd four months after meeting him. He very much wanted to marry me and I would have married anyone to get out of a life of sin.

He was a physically unattractive man, educationally handicapped but shared radical political beliefs and hatred of conventions. The morning after the ceremony I thought, "What have I done!"

Socially, intellectually, and culturally he was beneath me, and physically his habits were repulsive to me (though we were sexually agreeable). ("Personal Events")

When I asked Pauline why she married Lloyd, who by all accounts was a seriously unsavory character, she stated quite simply and profoundly that of course she married him, and even stayed with him after learning of his bigamy, because he was a *perfect reflection* of how she felt about herself at the time.[23]

Yet Pauline knew she could not stay in the marriage. She wrote in a letter to her mother (a letter she never sent), "I don't know what it is in me that is being starved in our marriage." She also acknowledged in that letter, despite her previous traditional notions of how much better off a woman was if she was married, "It's mostly lack of money that has wrecked the course of our lives. But we may as well accept the fact that it always will be. And I can earn more alone" (Correspondence, 12 November 1934).

When Pauline left Akron she secured a position as a clerk in the University Press office in Chapel Hill, North Carolina, and Lloyd accompanied her. Soon, however, she began proceedings to have her marriage annulled, a process that would take some time and during which she was ineligible for any teaching jobs.

Rebounding from her relationships first with Wilbur, then with Lloyd, Pauline determined once again to further her education. Still burned by the fact that she could not become a doctor, she once again considered medicine. Believing she was too old to undergo training to become a physician, she entered nurses training at Bellevue Hospital in New York City.

ENTERING NURSING AND FALLING IN LOVE

At Bellevue, Pauline met and fell in love with Sally, a senior nurse and entered into what was to be a three-year relationship with her. Pauline wrote the following in her diary:

> One half year [after leaving Lloyd] . . . I entered nurses' training. (I could not get a teaching job because of the situation with Lloyd; I had been fired at Akron because the board of that private school found his personality unsuited, and they had so written to Teachers College. No other agency would accept my registration, saying I was either over- or under-trained for their vacancies.)
>
> Almost immediately I entered into a homosexual relationship with my "big sister," a senior nurse. This relationship lasted three years. I entered into it with a feeling of complete and permanent defeat in masculine relationships. Sally's feeling for me was comforting both physically and emotionally for a matter of 4–5 months, and then I felt increasingly inadequate. We both played the devouring mother-role, although she was by far the more dominating personality.
>
> This relationship lasted three years. It was finally resolved completely when she began living with a married woman; I felt rejected. ("Personal Events")

Pauline's sense of "complete and permanent defeat in masculine relationships" drove her to a relationship with a woman. Interestingly, in the context of the 1940s her relationship with Sally took on a similar character to those she had had with Wilbur and Lloyd: all three were in the same sense "sinful" in that they were extramarital affairs. In addition, in all three she allowed herself to be used in various ways. In the first relationship, Pauline was used as an adulterous partner; in the second, she was used as an unknowing partner in a bigamous relationship; and, in the third, she was dominated by a mother figure who left her with feelings of inadequacy.

Meanwhile Pauline continued with her professional training and work. She was ill for six months in 1938 but was able to graduate with her entering class in August of the same year, with an average score of 92 percent. She worked as charge nurse on a medical floor, and later became night supervisor, through April 1939. She found the work exhausting, however, and jotted notes during that winter for a book that she would never complete, entitled *Night Float at Bellevue*.

Exhausted from working the night shift in nursing, Pauline decided to return to teaching and qualified as an English teacher in the New York City Public Schools. When a teaching vacancy arose in April 1939, she took the job teaching English at Boys High School in Brooklyn. She found teaching easier with its regular daytime work, more vacations, increased mental stimulation, and better pay. Pauline would only return to nursing for a minor portion of her remaining career, however she claimed that she would never have missed nursing and her nurses training for anything.

While teaching at Boys High School, Pauline entered Freudian analysis, likely an influence on her return to heterosexual relationships. Her analyst was Dr. Pauline Rosenthal, associated with Bellevue Hospital. Pauline would write years later, in an application to the Medical Society of Analytical Psychology, that she entered analysis to complete her professional training: "I had at that time completed training and received certification as a Registered Nurse. I had specialized in Psychiatric Nursing and had been led to analysis through a subjective need for further professional training."[24] Pauline recalled her experience in analysis:

> For the next three years I was a teacher of English in Brooklyn. I went into Freudian analysis for one year. I had a brief period of approximately three months of intense heterosexual experiences during this time. . . . I met Frederick and immediately entered upon a relationship with him. It was of only three months' duration but of great intensity. He was married and living with his wife, father of two children. He was a librarian in the school where I taught, a personable man, sensitive, well-educated cultured, above all—honest. We were completely compatible sexually (as he was not with his wife), as well as otherwise. The entire experience was very archetypal. ("Personal Events")

Frederick Meigs was a fellow teacher at Boys High School. Pauline saved dozens of notes and letters Frederick wrote her. The relationship was short-lived, indicating she had learned something about caring for herself. She recalled, "He told his wife of our relationship early, with a view to divorce from her. I decided not to continue the relations beyond a three month period unless he did decide to leave her. He did not so decide" ("Personal Events"). Simultaneously Pauline terminated her relationship with Frederick and ended her therapy sessions with Dr. Rosenthal. She said she really had been "related to Frederick" rather than the analyst, attempting to sort out her needs for and within relationships. When the relationship ended, she could see no further need for the therapy.

Recalling her years in nurses training and varied relationships, Pauline's reflection that, although brief, her experience with Frederick "was very archetypal" relates to her later understanding of the intrinsic inner balance of male and female. Pauline would come to see her life as not only an "outer" journey of material relationships, but also as the maturation of her "inner" journey as well. In 1996, as she approached her ninety-first birthday, she wrote a general "birthday" letter for her friends. In it, she wrote:

> Many people marvel, as I myself do, at my rather phenomenal memory of my own past life. During these recent years of reflection, I have begun to feel that the reason for my detailed memory of trivial incidents lies in the fact that they were not only outward events of which I retain knowledge but they were also personal events that to me were "real" inner events. I did not know about them; I experienced them. I did not know *about* them; I experienced them. Heretofore I was totally unaware of the "real" (spiritual) reality that links the material outer world and the inner world into a unified whole. The eventual chasm was not apparent at all. Without consciousness there is no pain; but unfortunately there is no pleasure either. What we don't know won't hurt us (?). But it won't help us, either. I reveled in experiences of all kinds, and consequently, I remember them.[25]

It would be many years before Pauline admitted publicly to being a lesbian or bisexual. Her tendency throughout her life was to philosophize about bisexuality and the soul rather than to proclaim out loud her sexual preferences.[26] One story she told that illustrates this view occurred after her retirement. She had attended a political meeting where some persons were advocating more visibility for the gay community. She said to one gay man privately that she did not understand why he and his friends wished to make public their sexuality. To illustrate her point, she said that she was a single, elderly woman. Should single, elderly women get together to talk about masturbation? Pauline broke into a grin, giggling as she delightedly reported his completely unexpected response to her, that, indeed, he thought that would be a wonderful idea.[27]

Chapter Three

War and Recovery

I Have No Time
I have no time for world peace groups:
I am a mother.
My days are spent with codliver oil and baths in the sun—
     So my son's sturdy limbs will better adorn
     A barbed barricade
     Somewhere afar, years to come, slain
     By a lad like himself.
I have no time to write Congressmen
Urging neutrality,
Indeed no. I am too busy cooking dried prunes—
     So the blood from his young chest
     Will redder and richer run
     As he drops lifeless in some foreign land,
     Protecting investments.
I have no time to study why wars are;
I am raising a son,
Cleaning, polishing, ironing white rompers.
     Then hypnotized by fife and drum,
     Stabbing with madness,
     Ripping out hearts with a bright bayonet,
     He will slaughter his brothers.
I have no time.
Margaret L. Truesdale, 1927

Pauline's courage for active protest in the face of a military buildup would take many years to formulate. Like her friend Margaret wrote some years before, Pauline would claim at the start of World War II, "I have no time," albeit for very different reasons. Pauline acknowledged to Margaret in a letter that she was deeply moved by her poem. Confronted with the reality of war and the exhaustive needs among many people around her brought on by the war, Pauline would face questions of meaning with more emphasis than she had for some time. The 1940s were passionate years, beginning with the desire to complete her schooling.

OCCUPATION AND PREOCCUPATIONS IN THE 1940S

The months immediately before the United States was abruptly drawn into World War II with the bombing of Pearl Harbor on December 7, 1941, would find Pauline working, searching, enjoying herself—not yet committed to any outside cause. These may have been some of the years in which she would later describe herself as having "wanted everything I saw, and a very restless, extroverted, tiring, tired, boring, *pointless* life it was at such times."[1] She did, however, begin one notable pointed effort at the time. In July of 1941, Pauline found herself back in school at Teachers College, finally determined to finish her doctorate.

Doing what she loved, studying, and having time to explore the city, Pauline enjoyed herself immensely during the summer of 1941. While on summer break from teaching at Boys High School in Brooklyn, she enrolled in three classes and studied for her matriculation exams, scheduled for August 2. She explained in a July 26 letter to a friend,

> No Ed. D. (yet). in fact, I have to matriculate over again, the last effort being outlawed with years. I'm attempting it next Sat., this effort being the one authentic excuse for all the other things not done.
>
>   I'm also taking three courses, and oddly enough liking them. Also auditing two and sometimes three others I'm way behind on my reading."[2]

And to her friend Win:

> I'm having a *swell* time this summer! I'm going to summer school. I went as an escape and an antidote, and I'm staying to learn and create. I've even gotten a dissertation topic after some 11 years, and I think I may write one in the course of the year. After which I shall be after a job on the West Coast, methinks! One reason I'm all hepped up is that if the dissertation gets done, it will be one that you will enjoy reading and will be proud of me that I think the things it will show. The topic at present reads: "What Boys High School's Curriculum Offers to its Maladjusted Students." (Correspondence, 25 July 1941)

Pauline wrote to her friend Jeannine: "Oddly enough I'm having a wonderful time this summer . . . I'm grateful to have found something that I can bite into

with a sense of accomplishment while my moon-baying is at its height. . ."
(Correspondence, 25 July 1941).

Pauline was, indeed, still recovering from her "moon-baying" and recovering from her relationship with Frederick, as she indicated in a letter to her friend John: "I thought once before, John dear, that I had caught my never-get-over. But obviously I was wrong, because here I am with Frederick in his place. I am hoping that he is not a never-get-over, either, though he seems to be sticking in the mind at the moment" (Correspondence, 25 July 1941).

Pauline planned to return home after her exams for a short visit to Spokane to see her mother. In the meantime, she enjoyed New York City and took every opportunity to enjoy herself and to learn about various people. In a series of letters Pauline wrote on July 25, she described an escapade the evening before when a professor at Teachers College, who had apparently taken her out on a date six years earlier, arrived at her door at 10:30 P.M. In spite of her exhaustion—she had just crawled into bed—she dressed and went out, not returning until 4:00 A.M. She wrote to her friend Margaret how that evening she witnessed a side of life she had not before: "he took me (we accidentally met two other people from T. C. [Teachers College]) . . . to Small's Paradise, which is a famous dive in Harlem" (Correspondence, 25 July 1941). There, along with other white Americans, Pauline witnessed Black dancers, or as she wrote, "Negro dancers," involved in dancing as she had never witnessed before. She also "discovered" the presence of transvestites, or "fairies." She wrote about the night to friends Hertha and Dale, interestingly mixing her gender references when describing the latter:

> Went to Small's Paradise. Have you been? In fact have you been?!!!
> Also have you read or seen "This Finer Shadow?" All the finer shadows arrived about three. We had run into another couple we knew in the meantime, and the other girl stared at one blonde beauty with a gardenia in its hair and a chin like a Neanderthal (mixed, I see, but so was he) so hard that he—it thumbed her nose at us and I feared trouble for a bit. God, what a world! I pine for the great simplicity. I'm taking a foul exam (have to repeat matriculations; I'm outlawed) next Sat. and after that I hope to see you and grouse in person. (Correspondence, 25 July 1941)

Pauline, as always, not only wanted to "grouse in person," but also wanted to discuss what was most meaningful in her life. Her professor apparently had in mind getting her to sleep with him. She mused on his shallow request, as well as on the consequences of her choice not to take him up on his offer. He was, after all, in her department and would be instrumental in her passing or failing exams. She further described her evening out: "I got back to the house at 4:00 A.M., and it is now 10:30, and I feel *foul*. I've come to the conclusion recently (only is it a conclusion?) that I'll take my sex along with marriage or not at all. . ." (Correspondence, 25 July 1941).

Pauline took the opportunity to reflect upon her date and to compare the past evening's exposure with what was really important. In her letter to Margaret, Pauline reflected:

> Your poem ["I Have No Time"] is appallingly good, darling. I'm so proud to know you. I'm so glad that the contrast is here when I run afoul of a night like last night. I'm so glad people I admire wholly like me, too. I'm so glad the people I like are so admirable. And I'm SO GLAD that I find it more fun to try to fit in there instead of living with shrugged shoulders. The guy last night is going through life to the inner tune of: We only live once (which I think is true, too. Very odd what different conclusions one can draw from the same premise!). (Correspondence, 25 July 1941)

RESISTANCE TO WAR

As she discussed meaning in her relationships, Pauline could not help but spend time reflecting about the profound implications of the war, as well as the reactions and actions of many of her friends. Pauline herself was absolutely committed to the notion of "democracy," yet she was unconvinced by the efforts of many around her to protect the same. Pauline's views remained leftist, although she did not at this time go so far as to consider herself a "communist." She repeatedly wrote in her letters her love for "patriotism and democracy and freedom."[3] She was convinced that much of the rhetoric she heard around her was not for true democracy, but fell short. To her mother, she wrote:

> One thing we'll doubtless talk about when we see each other (!) but I can't resist explaining a bit now. You say *"Surely* you are not even dreaming of being on the side of anything except Democracy." No, dear, I am planning to be on the side of democracy, all right, only I expect you and me to differ on which side that is. Maybe not, but I fear. So far, I've seem precious little democracy in this country among those that are yelling the loudest about it. (Correspondence, 25 July 1941)

Pauline was convinced of the hopelessly unstable situation of the world. She continued:

> I find myself in complete agreement that things are bad and are going to get worse. I am happy to report that for myself in person, however, I'm not quite so long-haired and upset about what I'm going to do, though no less definite.

Teachers College, I find, is all wrought up this summer about what is Democracy and what are the schools to do about it; and I can see how some of the people are clear-sighted but gutless, if I may use too crude a word; and others have courage but are muddle-headed (like the people who announce belligerently that *they* are ready to die for their countries—let them, if that's all they can contribute I say!), and a few are neither brave nor wise—or shall I say many in that class. But a very few are very wise and very brave, and perhaps not oddly very happy and gay. (Correspondence, 25 July 1941)

Pauline was not ready to die for her country, yet she would increasingly be torn by what nobler contribution she herself ought to make. She wrote her personal but not political support to her friend Harold, who had chosen to enter military service:

Look! I'm writing! And your letter is dated July 15th. One would think I had contributed to the Order of Draftee's Mothers, or Organization to Promote Defenders or whatever it is. But I ain't. I'm writing because I like you, in spite of your getting yourself ruined in the army. (Correspondence, 25 July 1941)

Pauline did pass her doctoral examinations, and received tempered commendation from Professor H. L. Caswell in a letter to "Miss Thompson":

It seems to me that you are in the process of doing some important and worthwhile critical intellectual work and I hope that you will continue this process. While it so happens that you did not make a distinctive mark on the examinations, I consider this of minor importance in relation to the evidence in your notes that you are really grappling with important issues and problems of a basic sort. (Correspondence, 16 August 1941)

After a twenty-day bus trip from Chicago to San Francisco, Seattle, Spokane, and back to Chicago (flying to and from New York to Chicago), Pauline began work on her dissertation, determined not to get involved in the war effort just yet. To her friend Marie she wrote: "I couldn't think of joining the Red Cross. Sorry, but I wouldn't. I'm disgusted with the whole war. I wonder who is fighting who and why; read 'This Above All.' That's me" (Correspondence, 11 August 1941).

Following her trip, she returned to New York and was ill with bronchitis for a month. After recovering and returning to work, she wrote these reflections to Maurice, a friend:

I have finally, (I think it is finally, too) parted company with my CP [Communist Party] friends about the war. I've turned individualist about joining and belonging at last. . . . It seems to me as if the imminence of compulsion to have opinions about politics is bringing infinite latent variations of those opinions.

This election, for instance. I've talked my head off, and so have my friends and acquaintances and even strangers. . . . In brief, nobody's opinion is worth a damn about anything except your own, and it's no good except that it is your own. You know, 'tis a poor thing.

I get so furious at the obvious course of history. You know, prophets aren't killed or reviled because they're prophets—only because of what they prophesy. If I could see the course of history widening with each new sun, people might like me, but poor old Cassandra knowing that those who will be foul will be foul! This country and England trying so hard to let Germany just barely lose, and so scared that they may miscalculate and she'll just barely win instead— only if they can stall long enough, it won't matter because she and Russia will both be so attenuated neither can win. Ah, and then we'll rub our hands together and pick up the white man's burden! Gug. I wish I had the guts to immigrate to inner Brazil. (Correspondence, 3 November 1941)

Pauline was alarmed at the inflation of costs. Convinced the economy would worsen as the possibility of war increased, she felt it would be better to have material goods than money in the bank. In numerous letters, she encouraged her mother to spend her money now and buy things for herself: "I'm *still* worried about your not spending your present cash for future goods" (Correspondence, 2 December 1941). Pauline sent her mother many gifts for Christmas in December of 1941, including a toaster and clothing. Pauline bought herself clothing and essential appliances.

When the war did come, Pauline wrote to her friend Charles: "Although I have been expecting the war for years now, it is something of a blow when it comes. My little English 2's brought in the news eighth period today, and we spent the period discussing it. They were very well informed" (Correspondence, 9 December 1941). Pauline was not yet ready to assist efforts to support the war, but was feeling a need for change. In November, she had written to Margaret that she was terribly unhappy in her work at Boys High School, and she considered the answer might be to return to the West coast (Correspondence, 17 November 1941).

In the meantime, she received permission to utilize records at Boys High School for her dissertation research. By December, she turned her attention to her dissertation as she was becoming exhausted and frustrated with her teaching, where the teachers were being asked to do more work with less breaks, as she wrote in a series of letters to friends on the second of December. In this letter to her friend Eugene, Pauline explained: "I'm so sick and tired of my job at Boys High School, Brooklyn, at this particular moment in history that I can hardly bear it. I am writing letters for a minute or two instead of correcting some of the 11 sets of papers that confront me" (Correspondence, 2 December 1941).

The teachers had just been given heavier teaching loads, the number of minutes allotted each class had been lessened by five minutes, and the office space had been reduced, all quite undemocratically. Pauline wrote of all the things she was being asked to do with her time, and added in her letter to Eugene, "and committee meetings on Practical Democracy in Ed. [present the] Crowning irony." Her friend Arthur replied after receiving a similar letter from Pauline: "With those doings of yours at the school, you sure are a phenomenon to me. Wish we could have talked over further those & related matters—let me know, will you, if there are any more developments in l'affaire Thompson."[4]

With the advent of direct U.S. involvement in the war, Pauline felt not only too busy, but overwhelmed with the needs of her students, needs she felt she could not fulfill. She found the lower-class, largely African-American neighborhood in which Boys School was situated a difficult place in which to promote democracy and the ideal of a land of opportunity. In a letter to friend Charles, she wrote of the boys she tutored:

It is particularly hard this term because I have a Remedial class that simply rends me asunder. I am so *sorry* for them, and they are so hateful. I ponder over every grade; they all need psycho-analysts and they none need any of the tripe our school offers them. . . . We have 38 or some such number of nationalities in our school, and a large and increasing Negro [sic] population. [Not to mention] Jewish prejudice. I have one psycho [sic] case, half Japanese, God help us all after today; he was bad enough before. . . . My instincts are right [in dealing with the student's needs], and I have more than average information, but I haven't had enough experience, the set-up is all wrong, and I'm not always sufficiently stable myself. (Correspondence, 9 December 1941)

By the end of 1941, Pauline, feeling inadequate to deal with the needs of her students while constrained by the time and budget cuts under which she worked, finally considered what her contribution to the war effort and the fight for democracy might look like. She wrote to her friend Winifred:

I have not gone to war yet, but I am in a state of considerable indecision as to how I feel. I was going to quote to you from a very sensible and interesting letter of Harold Richardson's, but on second thought I think I'll lend it to you. I'm torn between his feeling and one of rage that I'm being bull-dozed into another imperialistic embroilment. Stuart Chase makes an odd point in a January Readers Digest article: either this is a Power Politics war (which he views with tolerance if not enthusiasm) or it is a total war with the enforcement of democracy on the world as our aim (of which he said, "God help us all").

If it's Power Politics, thank you, I wouldn't be having any. I decided that years ago and I still agree with myself. But if it's total war, and I incline to think it is, then what? God help us all, indeed, yes, but help us do what? It's easy for the Moriarties, but you and I are made of more thoughtful stuff if not sterner. (Correspondence, 30 December 1941)

Pauline's being made of "more thoughtful stuff" would guarantee that she would attempt to make her contribution to the fight for democracy and would move on to seek meaningful work through which to do so.

JOINING THE WAR EFFORT

Early in 1942, Pauline took a post as a psychiatric nurse with the Migratory Farm Worker's Health Program. She took a leave of absence from teaching as well as taking time off from her dissertation studies. Work in the farm labor camps was both a way to leave the teaching job that she had grown to find less and less satisfactory and a way to become involved at least indirectly in the war effort. She worked in several camps for migrant laborers set up by the USDA Farm Security Administration to encourage those who were previously unemployed to migrate to farms where work was available due to the many male farm workers leaving for war.

Pauline worked as a senior nurse at farm labor camps in New York, Florida, Idaho, and Oregon.[5] Samples of her clinical reports, noting vast problems from alcoholism to infectious diseases, chronicle the lack of privacy and services available to nurses as well as Pauline's frustration at the focus on tertiary care at the expense of overall public health. She noted the connections between the health of the "social group from which the camp population is drawn" and the health problems she routinely saw: "My sense of haste and frustration exists insofar as I tend colds, fevers, female ailments, infections, minor accidents the livelong day, and all the time an immunization, teaching, and building program is calling."[6]

After more than a year, Pauline determined not to continue in the farm labor camps and decided to enlist in the Army as a nurse. In October of 1943, Pauline mused again on how to help the war effort when she believed that most efforts toward a solution—like those of addressing public health by the farm labor effort—fell short of what was really needed.

The decision to work as a nurse in the Army came with considerable reconsideration of her professional life. In preparation for enlistment, she was sorting out papers and discovered she had written on an old envelope a list of the professional positions she had held. As she recopied the list, she realized she had finally come to peace with her inability to become a doctor and no longer desired such a profession. The positions she listed included being a student, an English teacher, a secretary, a nurse, a librarian, a teacher of both elementary and high school, and work in social service. She also listed her ardent beliefs encompassing not just psychiatry and equality of educational opportunities for all, but world peace, free trade, a social economy, and widely available public health.[7]

On her twenty-ninth birthday, March 7, 1944, Pauline entered the Army at the rank of captain and worked as a general duty nurse until March 14, 1946. Her record of service describes her actual duties:

> Served on overseas duty for 15 months with the 48th, 40th, 228th, 82nd and 74th General Hospitals in France. Was charge nurse of chest ward for 2 months, skin ward for 1 month, orthopedic ward 1 month and trench foot ward for 2 months. Supervised and assigned duties to 1 nurse, 4 medical corpsmen and 4 French civilians caring for patients. Relieved when head nurse was off duty for short periods.
>
> Completed 2½ weeks course at Chief Nurses School at Medical Service School Center in Le Maris, France. Completed 120 hours course with Army Education Program in Settlement House Work.[8]

Pauline's work with the Army began in a hospital as psychiatric nurse in California. She wrote to her mother, whom she always addressed endearingly as "darling" or "my beloved," that she was weary from working with very difficult patients. She wrote, "It is a horrible kind of Wonderland and this little Alice grows more interested in sociology and more sold on socialism every day she lives."[9] Pauline also wrote many letters to her friend Win, who wrote back that she was profoundly moved by Pauline's descriptions of the men she took care of, encouraging Pauline to continue her work with a generous heart and the hope that the war would soon end.[10]

Pauline's entries in her diary from August to September 1944 indicate she spent most of her time working. On her time off, she found it difficult not to be too bored, spending much time reading. She would, of course, find boredom a thing of the past as she aged. She was actually relieved to find herself less interested in going to bars than in her earlier years. She felt she was maturing, no longer seeking meaning where there was no meaning.[11]

On August 29, Pauline discovered she would be transferred overseas. While on duty in France, Pauline met and began what was to be a long-term relationship with Lu Bassett, another female nurse. At one point Pauline and Lu were found in a "compromising position," or, as the colonel later stated, in a "compromising attitude." Another nurse came in to discover the two "reading the same book and lying on the same bed." Pauline was insulted by the suggestion that they would be caught in a compromising position. The two denied that there was a homosexual relationship between them, and they were therefore allowed to continue with active duty ("Personal Notes and Diary Pages"). In her journals, Pauline described her relationship with Lu as one in which Pauline took mercy upon Lu. She wrote that her senior officer, Major Bukky, the chief nurse, did not understand Pauline's role in Lu's life. Pauline wrote, "I figured overseas that if I could keep Lu on duty and out of bed it would be like supplying two extra people to the war effort."[12]

Once Pauline was relieved from active duty, she would again pursue studies and settle into a variety of psychology and teaching jobs. She would play less of the role of the fool, and would begin to delve deeper into her own inner psyche, after all these years turning her gaze inward.

Figure 2.   Paper doll sketch of Pauline E. Thompson teaching class, 1950

Chapter Four

Post-War Analysis

I share . . . [my memories] because I want to affirm as publicly as possible the value of one's past as the foundation of one's present.

Pauline E. Thompson, "Album Cover"

There is a fine old story about a student who came to a rabbi and said, "In the olden days there were men who saw the face of God. Why don't they anymore?" The rabbi replied, "Because nowadays no one can stoop so low."
One must stoop a little lower in order to fetch water from the stream.

Carl G. Jung, Memories, *Dreams and Reflections*

Pauline's "outer life" continued to follow a strong academic and professional pattern. After her service in France, Pauline completed her Doctorate of Education in 1947 at Columbia and, with her partner Lu, moved to Berkeley, California. They lived in a basement apartment at the home of Pauline's long-time friend, Margaret Truesdale Gibbs. Margaret's daughter, Carol, a young child at the time, recalls that she was told stories by her parents about Pauline's long-distance engagement to a man to cover up the lesbian relationship between Lu and Pauline.[1] After several years, Lu and Pauline bought a house together, and Pauline was hired as the first school psychologist in the Berkeley public school system. Shortly after beginning this work, she attended a talk by a female Jungian analyst, Dr. Renée Brand. Subsequently, Pauline and Dr. Brand corresponded regarding a case they shared an interest in. Soon, by October of 1948, Pauline herself entered Jungian analysis with Dr. Brand.[2]

47

"OUTER" EVENTS:
EDUCATIONAL, POSTDOCTORAL, VOCATIONAL

Pauline indicated in her writing that she loved her work with the Berkeley public school system. She very much enjoyed the children with whom she worked. But her relationships grew less stable. By 1950 while working for the Berkeley school system and still living with Lu, Pauline met Les and began a secret love affair with him. When she met Les, Pauline lived in fear for some time that Lu would discover her birth control devise and learn she had a male lover. Soon, however, she stopped the charade, hoping both Lu and Les could reconcile to sharing her. Les, however, wanted to marry her. Lu, on the other hand, was quite hurt.

It was during this time that Pauline's mother, Ida, came to live with Pauline and Lu. By 1951 Pauline and Lu could not reconcile their differences, and Lu moved out of the home they had bought together. Shortly after Lu left, Ida died in early March 1951. Several years later, Pauline later wrote that she felt guilty she had not been more attentive to her mother in the last months of Ida's life. She reflected upon her relationship with her mother in a journal entry addressed to Renée:

> And wonderful-daughter? Part of the time, Renée, part of the time. Not when she died. I never did share my tears and my guilt and my sorrow with you when she died. Not the way it really was. I was a bitch to mother after I let Lu in, Renée. . . .
>
> I keep contrasting her death with grandmother's. Mother was there, helping her sit up, helping her life down, sending for a drink, *sending* out for a doctor (not going out to the phone for five minutes—mother died in 25 minutes from the time I heard her call). Grandmother sat up and looked into the face of God. You could see her do it (dad was there, too, and I was there—lucky I to see such a wonderful release of life, embrace of death). But mother and I were lying like idiots—mother scared to death, "I hated to call you"—I not even admitting to myself that she was very sick: "You'll be all right in a minute," ("What shall I wear today; it's five o'clock am; God, how tired I am"), and then bingo, she is already cold, staring with cold eyes and a disapproving buttoned-up suffering patient rejecting rejected face.
>
> She wanted me to say I loved her, and I wouldn't. . . . [3]

After her mother's death, Pauline found herself increasingly lonely and dissatisfied with human relationships. She lived alone, except for her cat, Libby, to whom she wrote several dozen pages of poetry.[4]

In 1952, Pauline determined that she would like to pursue training as a Jungian analyst rather than simply continue to practice clinical work as she was doing in the Berkeley school system. Having received membership in the

American Psychological Association in February 1951, she subsequently applied for membership in the California State Psychological Association and the Medical Society of Analytical Psychology. She received word that she was elected to membership in the former on May 28, 1953. However, she was denied membership in the latter. In a letter dated April 7, 1952, she was informed that her academic qualifications did not conform to the required Ph.D. in clinical and abnormal psychology. Further, in a letter dated May 9, 1952, one month later, she was told that the Medical Society could not justify further training "with the expectation of becoming an analyst," a request she had apparently made upon receipt of her initial rejection letter.[5]

Pauline's reflection papers indicate she knew that her educational background was not appropriate for clinical psychology. She struggled with whether she should pursue additional studies in psychology, or simply admit that her role was to remain an educational clinical consultant in psychology. The outright rejection of her application to pursue training in Jungian psychology must have been a blow to Pauline, who was more enthralled as time wore on with the centrality of the unconscious. She wrote in her application to the Medical Society of Analytical Psychology the difference, as she saw it, between the practices of clinical and analytical psychology:

> Clinical psychology is psychology on a human practical level, dealing with people, as distinguished from theory; research; animal, experimental, and industrial psychologies, etc. As such it is basic to the study and/or practice of Analytical Psychology and can provide Analytical Psychology with relevant data.
>
> The most important difference between the two fields lies chiefly in the recognition of and dealing with the unconscious in Analytical Psychology. ("Correspondence, January 1952—May 1953")

Pauline would struggle with this question of whether to become a Jungian analyst until the year of her retirement.[6] She engaged in postdoctoral work to aid her with her professional quandary. From 1947 to 1948 and again in 1951, she engaged in further study in clinical psychology at San Francisco State College. From 1948 to 1949 she held a postdoctoral position at the University of California in educational psychology ("Correspondence and Application"). She was regularly invited to lectures sponsored by the Analytical Psychology Club of San Francisco and various other organizations, such as to one by Jolande Jacobi, member of the C. G. Jung Institute of Zurich on October 10, 1953. She had previously audited seminars by such Jungian scholars as Dr. John Perry and Dr. James Whitney.[7]

Pauline was not granted tenure by the Berkeley public schools, a decision she had anxiously awaited. By the spring of 1953 she had shifted her job position. She was hired as Dean of Girls at California School for the Blind. In her May 1953 journal notes, she asked herself both whether she should quit her job (even without another) and whether she should sell the house she still owned with Lu, who was by then living with another lover.[8] Pauline seemed to enjoy the girls with whom she worked at the time. After having been away and returning to the school on one occasion, she wrote:

> Good to be back, too.
> The kids all rushed out to greet me,
> And kissed me and petted me.
> Patsy went away finally;
> Then someone knocked—
> Patsy with a chocolate kiss. (Dreams, 22 March 1953)

In 1954, Pauline left the School for the Blind and took a position teaching in Daly City, California. Pauline moonlighted as a psychologist, with three patients at one time.[9] In April, 1955, she put her house up for sale, hoping to begin a new life in another home. Pauline's writings indicate she had her heart set on buying another house while her analyst, Renée, was questioning why she would want the sole responsibility of ownership (Dreams, 8 April 1955).

Meanwhile, Pauline shared an apartment with a woman, Lee, who appears to have been both a lover and a friend. Pauline wrote of a troubled relationship with Lee, indicating she missed having a man in her life. She mused upon whether a man would want to "take on the hazards of relationship with one woman who was already living with another one" (Dreams, 5 March 1955). By June, after some months of living together, she asked Lee to leave (Dreams, 3 June 1955). She assessed her financial situation and determined that with life insurance and the ability to qualify for a VA loan, she would buy a house in San Francisco. By August, she had moved into her new home.[10]

In 1962, Pauline took a leave of her Jungian analytic sessions and embarked upon a world tour. With the support of her friends, Pauline seems to have come to some decision that she must not just sit and wonder about her profession, but take some of her income to travel. Optimistically, she saw her salary as included in a "high salary bracket."[11] She was tired of settling as a seventh-grade teacher, a position she saw as beneath her, and wrote that, after all, she was unsure she was a good teacher at all.[12] Pauline took a six-month leave from her position and began a trip around the world. Letters between her and her cousin Muriel, as well as her analyst Renée, indicate she visited Japan, Taiwan, Manila, Cambodia, Saigon, Singapore, Indonesia, Tasmania, Melbourne, New Zealand, Calcutta, and Spain. In spite of misgivings she experienced while in Asia of America's "general unpreparedness and inefficiency" in the face of world tensions, Pauline wrote of her absolute pride in America.

Pauline had hoped to return home with new knowledge enough to begin yet another career, as a teacher of social studies.[13] She determined instead, however, upon returning to America, that she would not begin a new career. Nor would she resume Jungian analysis. She felt comfortable with what had grown into a very dear friendship with her former analyst, a friendship she would maintain until Renée's death in 1980. Pauline began to contemplate retiring at the end of the year.

"INNER" EVENTS: JUNGIAN ANALYSIS

The decision to stop analysis followed a long progression during which, parallel to her "outer" professional path, Pauline experienced much "inner" turmoil and transformation. She was beginning to see she needed to take control of her own personal and inner life, her own loves, and both the negative and the positive aspects of her nature. What she began to discover consciously was, as Jung described, that she needed to "stoop a little lower" by facing her past dependencies in order to discover wisdom.[14] Pauline began to understand she needed to face her "shadow," or the parts of herself she had hidden both from herself and others. And she recalled the metaphor of Aldebaran who was cursed to live a fool's life. Pauline acknowledged that sustaining wisdom would emerge only with the recognition of what a "damn fool" she had been.[15] This transformation to making meaning out of her past did not occur over night for Pauline, however. The woman who easily gave over control to others remained for some time.

Pauline reflected upon Lu's reaction when she learned Pauline was having an affair with Les, the man who had been the catalyst to Pauline's breakup with Lu. Pauline began one entry in her 1950 dreams and associations journal as a letter to Lu written the tenth of March, after Lu had already moved out:

>Oh, Lu, how cold my heart.
>I speak the words about you to our friends.
>I plan anew to write.
>But what to say?
>Between us all that was
>Now seems dead and gone. . . .
>
>It is true that I have loved unworthy men.
>Including the one who started all our conflict.
>But I could not stop loving him to suit your firm demands. . . .
>
>You would not give me time.
>"Choose now," you said.

You would not give me trial.
"He can't come in, for this is my home, too."
All's said and done.
You were right. I agree.

Pauline ended her entry with "I love you." But this last remark was not directed toward Lu, nor even toward Les. Pauline shifted her addressee and wrote instead, "I love you, Renée." Pauline, in fact, became completely infatuated with her analyst, Renée Brand. In 1950 she suspected the whole reason for entering analysis was this infatuation. She continued:

And now is Renée.
You [Lu] were right there, too.
A complicated game
Wherein I denied and lied about my motives for analysis
But you divined my real feelings, even so,
Before I did, myself.

Hundreds of Pauline's journals were written in the form of love letters to Renée, letters that are frustrated, poetic, even erotic. An entry in her dreams and associations journal written the next morning, March 11, for example, begins:

Renée, my dear,
My light and guide, my bulwark and my strength,
You are now become the living sacrifice to bear the burden of my love.

At one point, Pauline realistically likened her love for Renée to the "school-girl crush" she had actually had for a girl who was "best in sports" as well as in "scholarship, in looks, in leadership," and who crushed her with rejection. She was thankful that Renée, in contrast, "met my test" and "showed your love," thus not rejecting Pauline's love crush. She referred to Renée variously throughout her reflection papers, addressing her as "my mirror," "my mother," "my love," "my lover," "dearest," "my darling" and "Deliverer."[16] Later, in 1992, Pauline described her writings during those years as "love poems" to Renée Brand.[17]

Pauline presumably gave these entries (often written daily) to Renée. Renée and Pauline did not have an affair, although it is clear from Pauline's writings that she passionately coveted one. Her infatuation was a result most of all of her undying gratefulness that, through their analytic sessions, Renée helped Pauline to begin to find her way out of a pattern of relinquishing power to others unworthy of her in relationships. Pauline equated these sessions with intimacy, and her love letters to Renée indicate she viewed her an-

alyst with a sense of absolute perfection. At one point, Pauline was in analysis daily (at a $10 an hour fee) but eventually cut her sessions down to weekly
(Dreams, June 1955). This love for Renée would one day be reflected in a recovery of Pauline's inner wisdom and strength, or in Jungian terms, her au-
thentic Self. Indeed throughout these many years of analysis she would recover belief in her religion and her purpose for living. She summed up much
of her frustration after many years in this reflection addressed to Renée:

> Knowledge is not enough.
> I tried to learn their teachings. In many schools.
> I studied hard.
> I was no scholar (though many thought me so
> And confused me by taking my hunger for conceit).
> I know I was no scholar
> For they had much more to teach which I had no stomach to learn.
> The teachings lay like ashes on my tongue,
> And the more I learned the bitterer ran the lye.
> I tried to eat and was not fed.
>
> And then you came. . . .
>
> I knocked and knocked
> And knocked.
> I bruised my head against the walls
> And my hands beat bloody on the door.
> Now at long last is a growing light.
> The door is opening
> And I am tentatively finding the way to my own heart.
> (Dreams, "To Renée," 25 February 1950)

Pauline came to learn that she had relinquished power and control to others, reacting rather than acting throughout the years. She wrote: "Shall I get
back at last all that I lost from B to Z with all the others whose 'A' I wrongly
estimated? Maybe not. This intuition . . . with the other [men I have loved],
it was: 'Not that love went, but that it went in little ways'" (Dreams, 2 May,
1950). She listed the men with whom she had affairs through the years and
concluded that "these men were second-rate" (Dreams, 6 April 1950). She realized she was moving on to embrace a new freedom, the knowledge of who
she was apart from them. It would be, she recognized, a lonely journey:

> Yes, I know. It's not a question of better vs. worse.
> I know that in my mind.
> But in my heart,
> in my heart there fester and infect,
> There sicken and distemper,

My unborn children, the evenings by the fire,
The small domestic acts of welcome and of care,
The days and nights, the hours and deeds and years
I've spent alone, they having promised these things elsewhere
    before they promised me. . . .

And so I anguish on the phrases that should have been left out.
Not "Who am I to say, 'They're second-rate'?"—
Nor "Who am I to be so different?"
Just: "Who am I?" Period. (Dreams, 28 May 1950)

Pauline continued on September first of the same year: "I suppose I've never known any of the men I've loved, because that would involve an integration of their characteristics into a whole picture. And I couldn't see an integrated human being, because I wasn't integrated myself?"[18]

Pauline began this slow journey of integration, one she had unconsciously started many years before through her analysis. She surmised a pattern wherein she relinquished control at a very young age. She wrote:

I must write quickly, quickly,
Lest it fade:
When I was five, mother first committed against me
The crimes long since visited on her.
What she did or how she did
I remember not—as yet—
But what it must have been I feel
With that inner conviction and authority
I am beginning to trust, even in myself. (Dreams, 6 April 1950)

Pauline recalled the following occurrence around age five, during which she made the discovery that she could not do what her mother said and what Pauline wished at the same time. She had been playing with the neighbor children when one of the girls elder brothers came by and scared the young girls. There ensued a lot of tattling and name-calling, following which Pauline wrote she declared to her mother that "I wasn't going to play with Harriet again as long as I lived. Not ever. 'Oh, yes, you are,' said mother." Pauline continued:

So in front of all the collective [visiting relatives], I finally tried to close the incident by declaring my intentions despite mother's prophecy: "Mother, I can't do what you say and what I say both."

Mother did close the incident by telling me that I couldn't play with Harriet (or Eileen) for three days—of course that wouldn't matter if I wasn't ever going to anyway . . . but I shall always remember that miserable, interminable, BORED three days, each of the three of us bound to our own yards, Eileen the intermediary spending part of her time with her feet dangling over Harriet's low retaining wall, part of the time elbows on her lawn, feet extending full length into our driveway trying to touch the soles of my shoes as I did the same. (Dreams, 12 May 1950)

Pauline continued in her dream journal with the reflection, "It's a little dramatic, to say the least, to conclude that I've never trusted my own feelings since; but I would say that mother was devastatingly right and that I did what *she* said, after all." Pauline wrote of the wisdom of her mother in taking the action she did and referred to this incident in her papers:

Feelings of inferiority are undesirable.
Feelings of superiority are undesirable, too (though less a problem in this
    shadowed world!)

But feelings of inner authority are Good.
    These feelings are humble, but not inferior,
    Humble in their acknowledgment of everyone's equal inner authority.
Yes, feelings of inner authority are both good and humble;
But equally they are proud as well.
Proud because they are God in us, the kingdom of heaven within us,
The possibility that each of two billion living persons has equal entitlement to a
    sense of his own existence and his own moral judgment—
This is democratic politics, religious faith, economic security, social respect.

I said at five, "Mama, I can't do what I say and what you say both."
Then I complied. Also I rebelled.
Each rebellion followed by more and guiltier giving in
And further shutting off myself.
I lacked inner authority.
I lacked it thoroughly. Earlier? Now? Always?
I thought of myself, in fact, all individuals,
As products of interplay of forces—not as unique organisms. . . .

But miracle of that which I mistook:
I am not forced to comply always.
I lacked inner authority; I compliantly complied.
The still, small voice of God I would not, could not hear,
Though in some years He thunders.
I could have done what *I* said—had *I* been someone else.
But I am not that I of five in 1950.
Now I comply less. I rebel less. I look and hearken within. . . .

Too many feelings of inferiority and too currently—
To know that they are extraneous to inner authority.
And to know that inner authority—denied at 5—can be earned at 45.

I know some meaning of late coming to the vineyard,
But I did not hope to get full pay in this! (Dreams, 20 April 1950)

Having arrived "late to the vineyard," Pauline began to shed her insecurity, developing both self-confidence and deeper religious convictions as a result of a dream she dreamt in 1954, her forty-ninth year. She found the dream she called "Bertha" rather puzzling at first, but it would remain in her thoughts and guide her for the rest of her life. She began her story of the dream:

I must start by giving background to my dream of Bertha by telling something of my religious life up to the age of late forty-nine. There is a crucial relevance. I would never have had this dream—I would now be somebody else dreaming other dreams and leading a different life—had it not been for an incident in my nineteenth year.

At age nineteen I lost my religion. In one sentence. I had grown up a sincere and dedicated Christian, Methodist in creed and ancestry, missionary-fervor in depth, converted at twelve in a revival meeting, . . . attended church "services" five times a week, "testified" in prayer meeting from twelve years on, took "instruction" (a voluntary act seldom engaged in by Methodists) followed by baptism nightly prayers on my knees in spite of roommates in my first college year. In short, I *believed*. All this was voluntary. I can prove to myself that my religiosity was entirely voluntary as shown by my church attendance.

I had my tonsils out one Friday afternoon after school when I was in the fourth grade. On the following Sunday I intended to walk to Sunday-school and was quite shocked when dad said no, I couldn't. I discovered that he was right. When I tried to walk to the front door, my knees shook uncontrollably. It was the first time I could remember being absent from church on Sunday, and usually for four services at that, sometimes five. People ask when I started going to church and I reply, "At age minus nine months."

All of this religious pattern evolved because I *believed*. I memorized the most verses of anyone and won the prize of a funny fat Bible, and I had thoughts about what I had memorized which I used as memory aids. Sometimes I wasn't sure what it was that I believed, but I believed it. "Believe on the Lord Jesus Christ and thou shalt be saved" was the biggest stumper: I didn't see how one could control a disbelief but decided that I was lucky in not having to try—besides, I didn't feel the need of being saved anyway—saved from what? The basis, foundation, and core of my belief was a real to me as my own body. ("Bertha Myself")

Pauline recalled the change in her belief in God that occurred when she was unable to pursue her medical studies:

Now I had to face an entire adaptation to a totally different future, not just to my immediate future. There followed years of various church attendances (a social groove), humanitarian ethics, even prayer, but nothing, ever, with a sense of relationship to any force larger than myself. I didn't value a concept, an approximation, an ideal. I wanted personal response. Response to *me*, Pauline Evelyn Thompson. "Jesus loves *me*," I had learned, had accepted as truth, as truth. Where was He? More than that. "*Was* He, at all?" Was it all metaphor? Was I to pray to a metaphor? Why did people pray at all? If there were no atheists in foxholes, why were humans so constructed that we were impelled to create and buy such a treacherous and uncertain bill of religious goods; and if the religion wasn't just a bill of goods, *where was He*?

I was not philosophizing or rationalizing. I was fighting for my spiritual existence. I continued to fight in a desultory hopeless fashion for years and years. ("Bertha Myself")

The dream that would move her spiritual journey from hopelessness to renewed hope occurred during the week of Thanksgiving, 1954:

I cannot say for sure if this burning struggle with God did actually culminate immediately precedent to the Bertha dream; it conceivably could have occurred at another time. But as I remember it, one evening outer events drove me to my knees. I gave up my pride and my self-control and my brave renunciations (by this time I was pretty proud of my ability to renounce!). I buried my face in mother's chair (she had died three years previously) as I knelt on the floor, and I prayed as never before or since for a "sign." I didn't really expect one, I know now. For one thing, I had learned about the Pharisee's wanting a sign, and Jesus said they had already had signs and didn't believe them so why give them another? So nothing happened. I prayed and I cried and I called out, "Are You *there*?" No insights, not even a thought. I got up and massaged my kneecaps and washed my face and went to bed.

When I awoke, I realized that I had dreamed. If I had not been recording and listening to all my dreams in those days, Bertha would never have emerged. I would not have remembered, or remembering, would not have experienced.

"Bertha" was the dream. All of it. A one-word dream. It made no sense; I remembered it because it made no sense. Why should I awaken aware of "Bertha"? . . . not a voice. Not a visual image. Not an idea. Just a word. The simple word "Bertha." In one of my beginnings was the word. . . .

I asked, "Are you *there*? Does anyone hear me?" And I dreamed Bertha. Or Bertha dreamed Bertha, or Bertha dreamed me. Or God dreamed Bertha in me. Or is God "only" "nothing but" a collective unconsciousness responding only as a bell is responsive when you tap it? Or are these all the same? No matter how I word it, God also saw me, and for me that is enough. ("Bertha Myself")

Pauline discovered the term "Bertha" had a two-fold meaning. Bertha means "bright," which Pauline immediately associated with the bright star of Epiphany in her "four stars" metaphor. Further, Bertha signifies the woman who the three Magi from the East ran across when they were on their journey from Jerusalem to Bethlehem to seek the newborn child. According to legend, Bertha begged them to wait, as she desired to finish her housekeeping task, but they could not. Although she followed them after finishing her work, she could not catch up. Ever since, it is said, she has been wandering the earth in search of the baby and in hope of the recurring Epiphany.

Bertha—Pauline learned from the work, among others, of Margaret Mead —is associated with Babushka, the Russian version of the Bertha myth, with Befana in Italy who brings children presents on the Twelfth night, the day of the Three Kings, as well as with Scandinavian and German mythology. This archetypal character has been traced back to the goddess Freia, goddess of love, housewifely accomplishments, the winter solstice, and the Twelfth night, as well as to Mother Goose, a spin-off of Freia.

Bertha's various stories represented Pauline's story: her wandering for many years in search of the child, in search of belief; her gifts to children along the way; her belated discovery that she had been on this journey all her life.

BRINGING SHADOWS TO LIGHT

Following the dream of "Bertha," Pauline became more serious in her determination to confront her "shadow side." She identified as part of that shadow side characteristics including procrastination, disorganization, lack of control, and professional uncertainty. With the discovery of Bertha, the housekeeper, housework became an important metaphor for examining Pauline's life and inner shadows.

In March 1953, as Pauline contemplated selling her home in Berkeley, she wrote that she was finally getting her house and books in order, both physically and spiritually (Correspondence, January 1952–May 1953). Once in her new home, however, she lamented, "Why do I consciously, deliberately fail to put my house in order?" (Dreams, 5 September 1955). She continued:

> I am able to face some [major shadow problems] that may *not* be resolved ever, at any rate, which are certainly unresolved at present. . . . The first shadow thing is my utterly appalling procrastination of things which *should* be done to the point where they *have* to be done—but I don't do them. I don't put first things first, or even thirty-first; I just muff them completely sometimes, I don't know why. It's a complex I've known about for years and years; but I've never called it by a name and looked at it and urgently wondered about it and wished not to have it. . . .
>
> Another [shadow problem] is related: to live in a mess. I get more or less organized sometimes, but it never lasts more than a week. (Dreams, 14 February 1955)

Recognizing she fell far short of being a neat housekeeper, Pauline found her-self again and again sitting in her home procrastinating housecleaning chores. She increasingly connected this with a similar tendency to procrastinate when it came to taking control of her inner life. Again in October she wrote of what a mess her house was (Dreams, 2 October 1955). At times, she found herself sitting in her house alone, writing, sipping a few drinks until she wrote, "It is Sunday, 4:30, and I am quite drunk and expect to get a bit more drunk" (Dreams, 6 January 1956). Six years later, she returned to this metaphor when, nearing the end of her years of analysis with Dr. Renée Brand, she wrote, "I've no idea what my inner house is like. . . ." She did acknowledge that Renée had helped her to know of the existence of her inner house when she said "You've saved my life."[19]

Pauline continued, naming further hidden sides of herself: "Another is that I have little and sometimes no control over my persona. . . ." And finally, she discovered a persistent pattern, obvious from an early age, having to do with her frustration at not being able to become first a medical doctor, and later a Jungian psychologist. She wrote:

Another shadow thing is the shadow of the working me, the shadow-woman who goes to work instead of me, the uncalled "calling." I don't really feel—at least, yet—at least, with sufficient grace and clarity—the need to become a child psychologist or a psychologist at all, or a psychotherapist. I don't feel it enough to know if this is it, for me. School psychologist should be it. . . . (Dreams, 4 March 1955)

She pondered her upcoming fiftieth birthday as she continued:

Monday, my God, I will be 50 years old. And what have I? . . . I've just counted back and counted back and *counted* back, and guess where I stopped. The 25th year of my life was one turning point; I had always thought it would be, and I was not surprised when the NYC opportunity arose. A quarter century of that external adap-tation that Jung talks about had taken place. I got my Master's degree and com-pleted three highly successful years of teaching in June and Sept. respectively; and went to NYC and fell in love—hopelessly, helplessly, archetypally, neurotically in love. And haven't been or done anything worth a damn since.

One quarter century to climb up from "humble beginnings" to a place which caused an acquaintance to comment on the gold spoon apparently in my mouth. The good, Christian, smart, scholarship, wonderful-daughter, well-trained, suc-cessful, hard-working girl, so *worthy*! Nuts!

And another quarter century to climb down again. (Dreams, 4 March 1955)

Pauline continued writing in her journal meant for Renée's eyes:

Well, I'll tell you, Renée, my redeemer. I'm again good, and I'm again Christ-ian, through no virtue of my own. (God had to hit me over the head with a brick before I'd listen, I who thought I was so pitifully receptive only fate was so silent and so evil!) And I guess I'm still smart. . . . Though if I'm smart, God help us all! (Dreams, 4 March 1955)

Pauline's attempts to recover early memories and hidden shadows in her past were accompanied by a growing certainty of the soul she had known at some level she was all along. Carl Jung wrote, "From the beginning I had a sense of destiny, as though my life was assigned to me by fate and had to be fulfilled."[20] He distinguished between an outer personality that was seen by others, and a second, inner nature, one that knew one's destiny and the truth about those around. He described his mother as having such a "twofold nature," the second of which he referred to as the "natural mind," or the "archaic nature."[21] Pauline discussed an inner recognition of such an "archaic nature," wherein her soul dwelled, at an early age. Pauline wrote many pages regarding her discovery that she had "lost her will" because her mother was too busy tending to others to allow Pauline to be herself. Pauline was discovering her "destiny" now, her "fate," as Jung referred to it, in the course of analysis. She waxed poetically over the emergence of her conscience:

I am late, very late in keeping my appointment.
I have never loitered or tarried.
But have rushed, banged, forced, hurtled myself onward.
However, I am late.
I have weighed apparent alternatives at the forks of many roads
And have chosen difficult journeys to the bitter end of each wrongly chosen
     cul de sac.
Blind alley. Impasse.
However fate had kept her hand on my shoulder. I did not allow her to guide my
     footsteps; I could not hear my heart.
Nevertheless, destiny—not once but many times—offered me new opportunities,
     allowed me again and again to re-affirm a faith that would not die in spite of all
     the bodies of evidence accumulated in the cul de sacs.

Though I am come late, late,
In graceless haste and confused repentance,
Fate has followed me along; destiny has tried to parallel my life and now at last
     it can.
I have had a rendezvous with life, and I have finally kept my date. . . .

Humility is for righteousness' sake; self-love and knowledge gives true direction.
My fate has been to live in darkness struggling toward the distant, ever-receding
     light.
Now my fate changes—oh, markedly. It is not threads to weave together, warp
     and woof blended.
In my strength, in my acknowledgment of my own fate,

Its own authenticity, in itself alters. I am becoming a new woman,
And I can now bear freedom, about which I am much concerned.
Humility can never have freedom, but authority can.
I am now the master of my fate, for I belong to it and it to me.
I can now set about to learn myself.
Never all of me, of course,
but more of me,
And therefore more of who I really am. (Dreams, "Humility," Thursday, 6 April
    1950)

Pauline wrote her journals in the form of letters. The addressee of those letters gradually shifted throughout Pauline's seventeen years of analysis. After ten years of writing letters to Renée, she began to address her letters to God and to "my soul."[22] She wrote at times as well, "Dear I Ching" when she had a question to ponder or a decision to make.[23] She made use of the I Ching throughout her analysis, when seeking answers to such questions as the nature of her relationship with her analyst or to how to deal with one of her troubled students. In 1957, she wrote letters to "Ben," a name she coined for her "animus." She wrote, "It is a bit childish of me (quite a bit) to have to write *to* somebody—even . . . to 'Ben' now. . ." (Dreams, 30 May, 1957). At any rate Pauline was finally discovering that "inner authority" she felt she was denied access to for so long. By October 1965, she was writing philosophical papers in lieu of reflective journals. She continued writing dream journals, but as personal journals rather than as letters.[24]

That Pauline finally broke from her dependence on her analyst is indicated by her failure to take the advice of Renée while taking her world tour in 1962. Pauline wrote to Renée of a sudden illness she experienced while in Japan. She experienced sudden hearing loss in one ear and discovered upon seeing several doctors that fifty-five percent of her hearing was lost in one ear due to thrombosis of the inner ear. Renée's response was to wonder whether this was an omen indicating Pauline should cut her travels short. She wrote this in the face of tensions in world politics, but she also reminded Pauline of a dream she had had before she left on her tour in which she fell flat on her face.

Pauline wrote her analyst in return that, after she had pondered her advice, she decided the dream was not a warning, but "merely prophetic." Pauline continued: "I think . . . that I am due to fall flat on my face, no matter where I am, and that it is a good thing and the sooner the quicker."[25]

These discoveries occurred through the process of analysis, where the past became a foundation for present strength, and unfolded through reflection. The past represented, as Adrienne Rich writes, "now the stone foundation, rockshelf further forming underneath everything that grows."[26] In 1992, when Pauline discovered her drawing of the star she had written about forty years later, she rejoiced. Pauline equated her unconscious image of the star with an image of a stone discussed by Jung. Pauline's star image occurred while Pauline's thoughts of the nature of self and God were consciously beginning to form. Indeed, the unconscious recovery of the star image in 1952 occurred simultaneously with Pauline's rediscovery of God. For Pauline, this discovery was an experiential one, and for more than the next forty years she would come to understand the myth and mystery of God as she came to understand the mythic journey she had been traveling for some time. She wrote: "I like putting it this way: it has not been my fate that has been adverse; I have been adverse to my fate. . . . ('Adverse' means literally 'turned away from.'). . . And in spite of all this, dear God, in spite of all this, my fate turns out to be— a child of God. God spoke to me in a dream" (Dreams, 8 February 1955). Pauline later summarized:

> I got lost at age 19. I became re-found at age 49. Now another 25 years have passed, and my life is still Epiphany. In our increasingly darkening world, the light shining 'round seems to me more and more miraculous. I no longer boggle at miracles. Indeed, I think I could not survive with out them in that inner world where Bertha is. Without her, I could not survive at all in any meaningful way. ("Bertha Myself")

In another essay, Pauline concluded:

> By the time Bertha (and I) finished our housekeeping, the star had reached and passed its apogee. . . .
> I had identified my finite self-imposed tasks with Bertha. Like her, I was thus destined to follow subsidiary roads and detours and wash-outs. For 40 years I, like Bertha, was lost. The wonder is—and was—ever to see the star again. I was 49 when I dreamed Bertha and again saw the star overhead. . . . Here, over 40 years later, is a miracle of Bertha's being given a second chance to follow the star to the new life. The child over whose crib the star had come to its maximum brilliance said, as an adult, "I have come to bring you life and to bring it more abundantly." That is its direction and its meaning and after 40 years of detours I find myself again consciously on the path. I now have a place on which to stand, and consequently a place from which to proceed. ("Saturn")

That "place on which to stand" would be a religious foundation and a growing wisdom Pauline would carry into her retirement.

Chapter Five

Retirement and Activism

I shall enter the darkness only so far as I can carry fresh roses.

Pauline E. Thompson, "Fresh Roses"

Pauline consciously embarked upon her new path through travel, further education, and time with friends. Soon after her retirement in 1966, Pauline had hoped to sponsor a visit to the United States by an Indonesian family she had met on a trip there in 1962. The sponsorship would mean little more than a signature on Pauline's part. In the end, however, only the teenager Evelyn Thio was able to come to the United States. Pauline did far more than offer her signature, writing to a friend that she turned into "a real in-loco-parentis mother of an 18-year-old foreign student." Pauline felt she may have gotten herself in too deep this time, but later admitted she felt useful having agreed to help Evelyn: "personal commitment is more rewarding than social commitment, both for self and society."[1] In order to help Evelyn finish high school, Pauline rented out her house in San Francisco and in July of that year went to Bellingham, Washington, to stay with her cousin Muriel Nelson, where Evelyn was enrolled at Bellingham High School.

FRIENDS AND TRAVEL

In the summer of 1967, Pauline and Evelyn returned to San Francisco after Evelyn graduated from high school. They lived in a house on Noe Street Pauline had assisted her friend Eleanor to purchase. Pauline, Evelyn, and her visiting mother lived in the small, crowded house on Noe St. Meanwhile, Pauline's rented house was vandalized by tenants, and she sold it. She bought her final home in San Francisco and moved in on the eve of Halloween. Pauline experienced some health problems during these years, and underwent surgery on her right eye in 1966 and 1968.

Fully recovered, Pauline spent the next few years engaged in extensive travel. In 1970, she went to Mexico, then again spent a summer in Bellingham with her cousin Muriel. She visited and cared for friends in Spokane and Portland, and in 1973 took a four-month winter tour of South America with Muriel. She returned to Bellingham to recover from a case of "walking pneumonia" she caught while on her trip.

Her inner search continued as she engaged in travel and exploration. In 1974, Pauline spent the summer in Spokane at the World's Fair, having received a season ticket courtesy of her friend, Spokane photographer Erna Bert Nelson. Her further travels in the 1970s took her to Vancouver, B.C., and various locations throughout Washington and Oregon. Pauline returned to Bellingham to take one course at Western Washington College in 1977, the same year WWC became Western Washington University. She ended up staying for two years, participating fully on campus and taking a full load of college courses at Fairhaven College of WWU. The course subjects included Bible, mythology, education, and literature.[2] When asked why she would engage in study at the age of seventy-two, Pauline later responded she had an insatiable curiosity about life.[3]

Pauline was not shy to share her political views or her growing certainty of injustice in the world. In her annual Christmas letter, she chronicled events of the previous year, as well as offering her opinion and philosophy on current political events. Pauline often said if people were to look at the Christmas letters she wrote for nearly sixty years, they would discover her thoughts were unconsciously far ahead of her awareness during any given year. Apparently, the letters were received with varying degrees of welcome by her friends. Pauline's 1973 Christmas letter began:

> Several of my friends have told me that they find the flavor of my Christmas form letters *pseudo*-cheerful and *pseudo*-personal: and they wish I wouldn't write them.
>
> So this year I thought I wouldn't. I thought I would just confess that for me 1973 has, by and large, been a bust. I feel my personal age this year, for the first time; and of course the outer scene has made the cheer more *pseudo*- with each passing day.
>
> But!—But last night I got to reading old Christmas cards, and suddenly the old magic is there. I am as full of the "spirit of Christmas" as ever. "The spirit of Christmas" is a Dickens' quote and if one and the same man could write "The Christmas Carol" *and* "Bleak House," "Oliver Twist," etc., I guess I can produce one cheery little letter once a year.[4]

The notation, "But!—" is a characteristic comment of Pauline's, who could not help but write about her current frustrations in a year when she felt American politics were a sham. Pauline's papers, in fact, include not just Christmas letters espousing her political and philosophical views, but also lengthy letters to various politicians, as well as letters to charitable organizations with explanations of why she might or might not consider contributing, considering their respective current investments, activities, and involvements. Pauline never simply responded "yes" or "no" to a questionnaire received in the mail but inserted her opinions in the tiny spaces provided between the lines. She continued her "cheery little letter" in December of 1973, the year of the Watergate hearings, with President Nixon still in office. Although she began by saying she did not know why she had been depressed, she quickly moved on to demonstrate that she knew exactly why . . . the cause being the current political climate:

I don't know why I've been so *infernally* depressed. I've been telling you for years that the world was going to hell in a basket. But, dammit, this year the world IS the basket. We aren't going any more: we've gone. We have the President —not just any man but our one and only *President!*—who believes in character assassination; anti-personnel bombs full of barbed plastic arrows for civilian populations (yes, I do consider their use genocide); international pollution—the very word: "defoliation;" lying; thieving; unimaginable (by me, that is) disloyalty to his former friends when they no longer serve his purposes:—you name it. And, finally, the topmost crime in a democracy: oligarchy. Oligarchy: "the state in which the power is vested in the few," and our *President* says sincerely, "I'm it.". . .

These thoughts are why I intended to skip this letter this year. These thoughts seem irrelevant at best, not to say downright, fantastically inappropriate.

But I got this out of a soap opera this morning: "This is a good idea, to clock happiness while it is happening." So I now add what I *also* think.

I think everything I've already written. But I *also* think that evil in high places (and in me and in you) is no new thing. And that my own individual, personal, unique, sole and only possession of my own individual, personal, unique, sole and only responses to evil is what my life is all about. And what all human life is all about. It *is* the kingdom of the spirit, in fact. And this glorious property of humanity entitles me to laugh, and dance, and crack jokes, and even over-eat on Christmas day with humble gratitude that that's how people are made. I can *choose*. And I choose to clock and remember happiness. ("Fresh Roses")

Pauline's letter demonstrated her uncanny ability, as she grew older, to see evil at face value, to rant and rave, to refuse to shrink from her anger—yet, at the same time, to value life in its fullness, including the love shared among friends and the joys of being a sentient human. Pauline understood that each person was on his or her own journey, and although Pauline railed at the evil in the world, she delighted in the individual journeys each person takes. She captured this as she continued her annual epistle:

> I'm ME and you are *you*. And I like you and I love you, and I like and love just as much as if this *were* the best of all possible worlds. Besides, I must say that it has been interesting. . . .
>
> I am frankly getting a little bored at how far degradation can go. But I'm not going to "wallow." I shall enter the darkness around me and *in* me only in so far as I can carry fresh roses. (This is my epigram for the year.)
>
> I shall enter the darkness only so far as I can carry fresh roses. And when the darkness gets too thick for me to cope, I'll go back for more fresh roses, and so, hopeful, render both worlds their due.
>
> You, my friends, are my most fresh roses. In fact, your latest gift is this Christmas itself, and I am truly grateful. I was getting pretty sick of myself. So to you my love and thanks for being, and my hopes for your happiness, too, in 1974. ("Fresh Roses")

Pauline would later describe her 1973 epigram, "I shall enter the darkness only so far as I can carry fresh roses," as her description of the state of her unconscious at the time, before she was fully aware of the workings of that unconscious Self.[5]

In 1980, Pauline attended a Thompson reunion on the U.S.-Canadian border, where seventy-five of the George Thompson progeny gathered. That same year, Pauline bought a second house in Bellingham, thinking one day she might live and garden there. Her friend and former analyst, Renée Brand, was quite ill with Alzheimer's disease, and Pauline assisted in locating a rest home for her in May. Renée died within the month. Pauline saw it as ironic that when she heard of Renée's death, she "was out of address on a trip to Death Valley, of all places," with her cousin Tom.[6]

When she returned to her home in San Francisco, she and her cousin Tom visited sites of San Francisco, and he stayed on for several weeks to help her begin renovation work on both the inside and outside of her home, which would take much of her time for many months to come.

QUAKERISM AND PEACEFUL PROTESTS

In San Francisco, Pauline settled into The Society of Friends, a faith community which she had begun attending when in her sixties. She never actually joined as a member, although she wrote about her desire to join at various points. She found the Quaker practice of silence consistent with her understanding of her own gnostic-like faith. She referred often in her writings of statements made when, after a period of silence, one of the Friends stood to speak from the heart. She recorded some of the statements she made when moved in a Meeting to do so. For Pauline, gnosis, or knowledge of God, arose from within a person and spread out, as does Quaker testimony in a Friends gathering, to affect all other corners of life.

Quakerism was a basis from which to express her growing theological convictions, as it did not insist upon creeds that as often exclude as include. For Pauline, Christianity contained truth, but not as a judgment for all people nor a condemnation of other people. She wrote:

> I have found the ideas in the Judeo-Christian Bible *for me* to be the most valuable collection of religious ideas that I personally have discovered. I am well aware of many other formulations. If my parents had been Islamic or Hebrew or Chinese or gypsy or scientists or whatever, I would probably orient my religious values around different images.[7]

As a Quaker, Pauline was committed to pacifism. This stance, and her belief that one needed to take personal responsibility, led her to participate in civil disobedience on more than one occasion. When in her late seventies, Pauline joined her Quaker friends in one of the semiannual peaceful protests at the Livermore nuclear facility in protest of nuclear weaponry. On this occasion, newspaper accounts describe her arrest with 649 other persons, all handcuffed and taken to prison at Santa Rosa. They were kept in a gymnasium facility until their release three days later. Pauline would be jailed for participating in nearly a dozen nonviolent protests from 1982 to 2000.[8]

Pauline came to understand that "peace" did not equal "comfort." She wrote in 1994:

> Now in my very old age, I am re-acquiring my childhood fascination with words. They reflect the evolutionary wisdom of the ages. They have a linear existence as arbitrary as our own life calendars. Some of my earlier words have developed characters far different from those of former years. One of the words that I used to treasure now irritates me beyond expression.
>
> God forbid that I should become *comfortable*. The human ability to adapt is about to do us in, permanently. To be comfortable when you should be acutely uncomfortable is a dangerous sin whose only conclusion is a comfortable death. I really don't know which is worse; undue pride or fatal complacency.[9]

Indeed, by the time she was taking courses in Bellingham during her retirement years, Pauline was firmly committed to peace activism. In her seventy-ninth year, she stood weekly in the cold winter dampness of coastal Washington to promote a nuclear freeze and participated in dozens of meetings and campaign endorsements. The front page of *The Bellingham Herald* featured articles entitled "Peace . . . when?" and "Nuclear freeze supporters quieter now, but intent on winning," accompanied by a photograph showing Pauline among a group of protestors outside a federal building in Bellingham.[10]

As the 1984 Presidential election neared and Ronald Reagan was at the height of his popularity, Pauline dedicated much of her life to the promotion of peace. Indeed, by 1984, Pauline felt personally called to peace activism and gave it her all. She had emerged from what she in various ways described as many pointless and selfish years, convinced of her obligation to promote peace for the world's people.

Most of the protests in which Pauline participated were held on Good Friday and Hiroshima Day (October 6) each year at Livermore Nuclear Laboratories. The protesters would arrive by 6:30 A.M. and hold a carefully orchestrated rally across from the Laboratory gates, where those who wished could address the gathered crowd. At the appointed time, six to twelve protestors at a time would step forward to face the police, who stood in a row in full riot gear. The police would read the protestors the "riot act," take them behind the line of police, handcuff them, and take them to wagons. Two friends, David Hartsough and Robert Levering, always accompanied Pauline during the protests. Levering wrote this recollection:

Each time we went to Livermore together I was inspired again by Pauline's Spirit and determination to speak and act for Peace and for all God's children. Increasing age and getting up at 5 A.M. were no deterrent to Pauline. Even the guards who arrested us caught the Spirit and treated Pauline as a child of god, and were always careful not to let us get separated while in custody. On many occasions Pauline shared with all those assembled at the Livermore Labs what the Spirit had led her to share and what had led her to the gates of that deadly place. Each time people were renewed in Spirit and felt here was a role model— a person who even at a very advanced age, still had a Strong Spirit and was determined to speak and act with her life for her beliefs.[11]

Hartsough recalled one of the last times they accompanied Pauline to Livermore. When they were handcuffed, Pauline was somehow separated from her friends. David turned around to see her standing with tears in her eyes. He saw that she was unsteady with her hands tied behind her back, and he convinced a guard to let him return to walk with her. He believed she was never fearful for her life, but only at that moment experienced the uncertainty of her frail body.

Pauline, he said, went into each protest knowing full well she might be jailed. Many protestors took part, but all were conscious of the careful orchestration between police and protestors. They counted on the protest to go smoothly. Pauline did not worry for herself at all but was concerned for all the people of the world who could be incinerated if nuclear weapons were ever used. She told of the time in 1982 she was arrested with over one thousand protestors. Her memories were fond ones of the young women she met and found herself counseling with while in jail together. Although the protestors believed strongly in the cause, David recalled that Pauline was the only one brave enough to give voice to what they all feared—that their heartfelt plea might be ignored by the powers that be. Each year she would declare she was not going to participate again, calling the protests a "ritual futility." But each year, she recalled, "I kept on protesting because I couldn't find an alternative."[12]

Pauline herself wrote of her plans to get arrested in 1987 at a protest against nuclear weaponry. Her writings indicate she was indeed arrested in 1987 and that she felt at peace concerning her inevitable arrest and even her possible death.[13] Pauline treasured some memories of her jail experiences. Dozens of women would be gathered around, and she would have opportunity to speak with single mothers and persons in less privileged social classes whom she otherwise would not meet.

In the early 1990s, Pauline accidentally fell down the stairway in her home. She experienced extreme pain following the accident and, to hear her tell it, received neglectful care in the hands of the Veterans Administration and under the administration of Medicare. She was first told, she recalled, that her pain was not all physical, and she felt treated as a silly old woman. She said, "I had fallen down an unlighted stairwell and thanks to the appalling ministrations of Medicare I almost died; five months later, it was discovered that I had broken my neck." For the next three years, she wore a neck brace most of the day and night.[14] Pauline suffered a broken hip in 1997 and was hospitalized several times for edema in her legs. During this time, though she slowed down physically, Pauline's spirit was not deterred. She found new anger toward the medical establishment due to what she saw as mistreatment of her injuries. That frustration only fueled her criticism at society.

In 1996, Pauline wrote of her intense anger at privatization, which she saw as relinquishing responsibility on the part of a democratic government, especially responsibility for poverty. By this time she had regained her faith in God, which became intricately intertwined with her understanding of her duty toward activism, embracing her brothers and sisters, and uniting her collective Self and her individuated self. Pauline wrote,

> I am suddenly no longer justified in feeling alone. In the last decade there have been fantastic developments of awarenesses. . . .

And now comes the basis of *my* anger. I am not stupid in the ways our so-called government operates. I have seen for the last half of my long life the stupidity of godlessness. I have seen the stupidity of the lives which seem to me to consist primarily of "eat, drink and be merry, for tomorrow we die." (And to not worry one moment for all your fellow creatures who have neither food nor drink nor cause for merriment, for they are dead already to any hope of merriment.)

My anger is beginning to be, more and more consciously, against myself. Why am I willing, after how many million, trillion, whatever years, to still go on politely saying no to our present social structure? . . .

I have been politely, *civil*ly disobedient for many years with such safety that my longest suffering consisted of three fascinating days in jail. Now I find that we have institutionalized acts of civil disobedience so that they have their ritual and their protocol and their dances between the "cause" and the citations. We are no longer news. We're just nuisances. . . .

I'm not trying to change the lousy world; I am trying to find new and better adjustments *within ME* to the world I live in. Poor world. Lucky me. Selah.[15]

Pauline believed firmly enough to risk her own life, yet withheld judgement regarding how or even whether others should make the same commitments. She wrote that because of the truth that "All men are created equal," and she went on to say, ". . . who are we to judge! It's none of our business who will stand and sit on the right hand of God." She noted, "I must recognize that my philosophy is hand tailored by me and for me and for me only."[16]

Pauline's was a philosophy that tied her with her brothers and sisters, including strangers, her mother since (and even more than before) her death, and countless ancestors and human beings of the past. She wrote:

Put it this way. I doubt from the evidence that [Newt] Gingrich is much upset at his inability to love the great impoverished unwashed. I find it equally difficult to love Gingrich. But I want to work at it because I am convinced that love is the only way.

I guess, in practical terms, that I am still totally without present capability of healing this split between my individual self and my collective self. I still have the task of being both sister and brother to my brother-and-sister others. ("The World is out of Joint")

On a range of issues from nuclear weapons, to racial diversity, to homelessness, Pauline viewed contemporary societal efforts to be inadequate. She felt current efforts at racial equality did not consider the complexity of the issues: "I see no possibility of real racial harmony in our existing social structure. Our aim reportedly is to see life steady and to see it whole . . . [but] if we create a mathematical climate in which "A" can only survive by enslaving non-A—in which non-A cannot even achieve survival, let alone wholeness" we create a structure that precludes equality.[17]

In 1994, Pauline participated in a demonstration to protest the plight of the homeless, which she called "everyone's disgrace," in San Francisco. The notice of her arrest indicates she was "lying prone" in a sleeping bag at Union Square Park. She refused, when given an opportunity to leave, and was arrested on June 14, 1994 ("Getting Arrested").

By 1996, at the age of ninety-one, Pauline wrote in her annual Christmas letter:

> Need I spell out how my political front also has changed? I shall still (or, rather, again) get arrested periodically for protesting political events, especially of course the *major* nuclear/germ warfare/arms production insanity at Livermore.
>
> But my main efforts for the rest of my time will be in behalf of a belated recognition that protesting is more or less a polite cop-out. *They* know I protest; and we both know they couldn't care less.[18]

Pauline later said that she saw protesting as a waste of time and did not intend to participate again. She continued, however, to write letters to politicians and organizations in attempts to make her politics and her anger heard. She continued in her 1996 Christmas letter:

> I finally have gotten it through my thick skull that I cannot *ever* counter/force physical force. The only way that can be done is to beat them at their own game, that is, to get more evil than they are. In short: "Power corrupts, and absolute power corrupts absolutely." The common excuse for blaming the Democratic party or the Conservatives or the greedy politicians—anybody but ourselves, everybody but ourselves—is that ourselves have not in 30,000 years or so come up with a *different* force. We tried Christianity, more or less, but it seems to be costing more than we are interested in possessing.
>
> Now I am finding *certainty* at last that I *like* Christianity better than I like Capitalism. And I *like* affirmation better than punitive laws. And I *like* do-gooders better than gangsters, and I *like* the Nation better than Vogue, and I *like* Bartok better than I like Elvis. I could go on all day.

Pauline turned this certainty into her writing. In the last decade of her life, Pauline formulated what one could loosely term a systematic theology. She wrote extensively on images of God and Christianity as well as on politics, peace and activism, good and evil, the feminine, astrology, and love.[19] Her writing occupied her time through the latter 1980s and the decade of the 1990s—resulting in essays filled with valuable insight for religion, women, and psychology.

Figure 3.   Star and Cross Drawing, Active Imagination Drawings by Pauline E. Thompson, 20 November 1950

Chapter Six

Religion and Relinking: Pauline's Theology

I somehow doubt that one can be a Christian at all if one is unable to deal with paradoxes.

Pauline E. Thompson, "Paradox"

Like Jung, I don't believe in God; I know.

Pauline E. Thompson, Christmas Letter 1996

Pauline came to the conclusion that the main project of her life was a religious one. Similarly, she saw the project of the man most influential in her life, Carl Jung, as one of seeking, and finding, the humanity of Jesus. She was angry at biographers writing on Jung when they omitted his deep religious conviction, and she claimed they were simply making money by taking advantage of Jung's death.[1] Pauline wrote:

Jung has defined religion as one's highest value; my religion is itself my highest value. The word "worship" and the word "worth" come from the same root. My religion has been very hard come by. I valued so many things I now consider false values. The harder it's come by, the more brilliant and durable and meaningful it becomes. ("My Cross")

Pauline defined "religion" in a 1996 birthday letter to friends as "re-linking." She saw being religious as similar to breathing, smelling, tasting or seeing. It was the experience of being connected to the "unseen world of the spirit" ("My Cross").

Following her "Bertha" dream and her reconversion to faith in God, Pauline returned to the religion of her ancestors, Christianity, for a context in which to understand God and to "supply the meaning" implicit in her faith.

73

This time, however, she did not see herself as a Christian holding the innocent beliefs of her literalist Methodist upbringing. This time, she sought the wisdom of Christian myth with the joy of a wayward child who has come home or a lost sheep that has been found.

By the time Pauline was in her late eighties, she wrote that she held a "strongly developed and deeply committed inner life as a Judeo-Christian (Christian of the gnostic school of belief rather than of Christianity as an historically institutionalized object)" ("Saturn"). Still a voracious reader and curious learner, several years later at age ninety Pauline would question this label of "gnosticism" yet retain its essence in describing her belief:

> Carl Jung in his turn has been spoken of as a Gnostic Christian, and I have thought that I also am a Gnostic Christian. Some of my recent readings lead me to repudiate this adjective, also. Be Gnosticism as it may, the unquestioned fact is that Jung—and I—are not the literal Christians who hope to achieve their travel guide through life by following a literal guidebook. ("My Cross")

Christianity became a metaphor for Pauline that applied to all times and all places. In a Christmas letter, Pauline discussed the first bright star that shone over the stable, lighting the way for the shepherds and the Three Kings to Jesus's birthplace. She wrote to her friends in an "Epiphany greeting," "Maybe this whole event is a belated fairy tale; maybe it never 'really' happened. No matter. There is no doubt whatsoever that it was—and is—a psychic spiritual reality." Pauline's reflection continued:

> Of course, especially to non-Christians (of whom I was one during the middle almost half of my lifetime) a relationship needs to be drawn between the spiritual meaning of the star and the spiritual meaning of the life of Jesus. What was so special about Him that we speak of Him in capital letters? So there was (or was not?) a star and other attendant miracles. So what?
>
> I have come to have an unshakable faith in the transcendence of the human spirit over time, space, motion, matter—over all physicality and mortality. And this transcendence is due to humanity's capacity to love:
> > "and the light was for all time,
> > and the love was for all men."
>
> Christmas is the celebration of our births as human beings. We are the only animals in nature endowed with consciousness of our selfhood, not only having egos, but *aware* of having egos. Epiphany celebrates our additional divining of our divinity. We have gifts of the spirit which lie far beyond our animal comprehension or our rational attainments, gifts which even transcend our own knowing.[2]

Pauline came to devote herself to Christianity in large part because it was her heritage. She wrote of the Judeo-Christian tradition:

My own adoption of Jewish tradition, the Jewish images of Jehovah, the Jewish tribal structure, the unique Jewish faith, in short begins, I think, with my picturing Abraham and his following as leaving the land of Ur to travel across a continent and settle in the land of Canaan. I think I picture that journey as the same journey my own ancestors made when they left Europe and later crossed from Maryland to settle finally on the Pacific Coast. Like from Ur to Canaan. Same ancestors, same journey. . . . (In any case, this is my image. Ur is no farther off or farther back, psychologically speaking, than my own grandfather). Where I stand today is on the new soil where my ancestors set up their Christian rituals more than a century ago. . . .

And they (my ancestors) must have had this same evaluation of themselves judging by the way they named their offspring. My family background was in the Puritan tradition, apparently. I had an Aunt Sarah and an Aunt Rachel and even an Aunt Elisheba. And an Uncle Joshua and an Uncle Ezra, not to mention Uncle Ebenezer.

So I find that with no effort of my own, indeed despite some negative resistive efforts, I am now a Judeo-Christian. Not a typical one. . . . ("My Cross")

ON GOD AND EVIL

In the last decade of Pauline's life as she formulated her comprehensive theological views, she came to embrace the reality of paradox as encompassing not only human conflict, but also God. Pauline believed life was filled with duality, and one must make choices. Yet, this choice was not a simple one as presented by right-wing Christians, but a continuous living with paradox.

She discussed the notion of how the Christian claim to be "the way" can be true, without claiming other religions to be false:

I have long stumbled over the problem of Christians' assertion that Christianity is the only way to God. I finally am satisfied with this assertion. It does *not* say that other religious approaches are not equally valid . . . it would be supreme ego—stupid at that—to feel that other creeds are not equally valuable. But the Christian religion seems to be the only one that embraces all the others (ideally) and then introduces the further concept that all individual souls individually and inseparably and universally share the soul—soulness—of the nameless all-God. ("Runyon/Ego")

As she struggled with the problem of Christianity as "the only way to God," Pauline also grappled with the problem of "right-wing" Christians. She wrote in 1995:

For nearly half a century, I have been striving to create a link between myself as a left-wing hard-core Christian and the right-wing Christians, but I still don't have the faintest idea how to do this. I have failed totally as a connecting link. I cannot even affiliate truly with *either* group.

One of my dearest friends, let's call her Louise, is a Quaker of long standing. Maybe she's a "born Quaker;" I myself am a more or less "convinced Quaker." I think that after a lifetime of pondering and seeking I have found someone at last who listened and who finally understood my point of view, even though she is unable to approve of my relationship with right-wingers. She caught me this morning in a violent conflict (not physical) with an Arab acquaintance whom I shall call Amat. Amat considers himself a Christian, and I have been trying to explain to myself as well as to her my extreme difficulty of adapting *my* Christianity to that of a "right-winger."

Of course, my relation to all right-wingers is conflictual. How come we speak of right and left wings as if the whole topic was a whole bird whose right and left wings were totally out of sync? . . .

I have come to feel with mounting passion the terror and rage and helplessness and general dissatisfaction with my Self that I still have not a clue as to how Jesus, in 1995, would deal with a chauvinistic right-winger. I find Amat completely selfish and incredibly chauvinistic. I said to him this morning, "This isn't the way to deal with me. We must learn to love each other." I was angry and helpless and quite incapable of appearing loving. Whether I was more angry or more helpless I do not know. Anyway, his literal response was, "I don't care."[3]

Pauline continued by saying she was convinced one could not call oneself a Christian and still say "I don't care." On the other hand, she admitted she had no idea of how to care. She was against violence, yet did not know another way. Her stumbling block with Amat was his view of her as inferior as a woman: how could they ever speak with mutual care? Yet she admitted she herself could be equally adamant in her position, as she continued her reflection on her meeting with Amat:

We even see our natural world only in terms of conflict. It should be our pleasure and our joy that we have the capacity to diversify everything, from a whole breath, yang and yin, to nuclear power in space. I feel that I perceive everything that I do perceive as a perception of this duality. And no matter how fanatic I may be (to put this issue in an individual context), I must recognize that however fanatic I become there will be an opposite fanatic on the same subject. ("Right and Left Wing Christians")

Pauline grew angry with those who called themselves Christian and acted as if, once redeemed, life is simply an easy party. One could not say, as she reported her acquaintance Amat as stating, "I don't care." Rather, one needed to make effort to care.

Pauline's views on the importance of Jesus's life departed from too concrete an interpretation. Jesus, rather, embodied a spirit to be emulated. She wrote:

My being brought up in the church, Christ's statements used to bother me like heck when I began growing away. Either he was a liar and imposter (Son of God) or it was true; the first judgment didn't seem to fit his character and total personality, and the second didn't fit with the external world as I saw it. I now think that He, too, was trying to fit the pattern of thought and semantics of his time, making a gigantic personification which the *more* (!) material-minded still accept literally to this day. ("Collected Letters Drafted")

Pauline was convinced the atonement of Jesus was not meant to be taken literally. She believed Jesus did not die on the cross simply so we could stand by and watch, redeemed:

We make a big deal out of Jesus' crucifixion. We fail to notice how many thousands—millions?—trillions? of other people have been crucified (in may ingenious ways besides the cross). The distinction that Jesus won is that we know he was making a point; it was *intentional*. It was person. It was consciously soul-saving. It had *meaning*.

I am angry that the best groups I know or know of do honor Jesus but stick at the point of living it out as He did. He earned that capital "H." He did save His soul, showing us how. We look on and see how it's done and how worthwhile it is and what a noble death. And we admire ourselves for looking! But it is part of a common creed that Jesus "died" for us; He did it so we don't have to.

I personally cannot buy this concept of "Savior." Whatever is bought—good or ill—has to be paid for, and if we don't pay our own bills someone else will have to do it. We have mortgaged our children already for how many generations to come! ("The World is Out of Joint")

Pauline felt that her past attempts for redemption and pardon for her past sins were conceited. She defined sin mainly as ignorance, omission and especially the "unconsciousness and/or denial of our own creativity . . . our major sin."[4] Her attempt to receive redemption did not allow her to stand by and watch Jesus climb a hill toward crucifixion for her. She explained that a Christian understands redemption as trying to pay back as one repays a pawn shop and, because he or she is unable to, someone else pays back for her or him.[5] Instead, Pauline argued we need to take personal responsibility for sin in the world. She was particularly concerned with nuclear proliferation and the ignoring of those in need of care in our society. The incarnation of Christ, she argued, was not an exclusive way to salvation, but a way of life. It was a way to follow, the way of Jesus's love for all. This way was not easy, nor did it contain "right" and "left" or a clear path. It was a complex path, filled with paradox.

Learning to be comfortable with dualism, with paradox, rather than assuming one can do away with it, was essential to Pauline. She wrote: "I feel that this problem of the containment of the opposites is fundamentally universal"

("Right and Left-Wing Christians"). Pauline discussed the connections between the words "paradox," "parable," and "parallel." On a life journey, it is not (as some Christians might have it) that there are "right" and "wrong" parallel paths or choices. Rather:

> Everything we have ever learned or done can be made untrue and meaningless and even death-dealing if it is out of harmony or context. Conversely, everything we have ever learned or done can be seen as meaningful experience insofar as we are willing to supply the meaning. . . .
>
> The parables of Jesus of Nazareth were all about the choices involved in dualism.
>
> I somehow doubt that one can be a Christian at all if one is unable to deal with paradoxes.[6]

Several dualisms were paramount to Pauline—including darkness (as unconsciousness) and light (as conscious awareness); darkness (as evil) and light (as love); meaninglessness and meaning; meaninglessness and synchronicity; ego and soul. Pauline utilized a deconstructive analysis and was interestingly ahead of her time in unconsciously mirroring some late twentieth-century postmodern philosophies when she insisted that the meaning of one thing is found in knowing its opposite.

One of the most interesting dualisms appeared in Pauline's understanding of the dark side of God, even the evil side of God, that enables one to understand a loving God. Pauline wrote:

> Most Christians do not recognize that when God created heaven He simultaneously and unavoidably created evil. Or I could equally say that when God gave humans the human property of being able to choose good or evil this very freedom of choice meant that if, like Mephistopheles, we say, "Evil, be thou good," that freedom creates the duality. We like to say that God is omniscient and omnipotent. True enough. We don't say that His son Lucifer is also conscious and potent and to many people more omniscient and omnipotent than God. If we could bring ourselves to admit the history and the power of evil, we would be infinitely more in the image of God.[7]

According to Pauline, God may be a lot of things, but God was not all-powerful. But that is not to say God was not "all." Pauline commented about a Quaker meeting that "for many weeks . . . has been concerning itself with increasing frequency about the nature of God." She reflected further upon recent discussion among the Friends:

> Last Sunday so many people spoke their own joys and their own griefs in such diverse ways that I found myself deeply impressed with the sense of the All-ness

of God. I realized God must necessarily, being All, accept all conflicts and op-
positions. If I am an anti-abortionist and you feel dedicated to what is currently
mis-called free-choice, God accepts us both equally. If your life is dedicated to
love of your fellow man and I am a criminal product of Watts, CA., God accepts
us equally. God is All. In fact, opposites form a continuum, and it is impossible
to see one end of a continuum unless one also images the other end. God sees
the whole line, however long, however short or faint. Einstein discovered that
space is curved, and any line, extended to its limit, becomes a circle, *any* point
on the circumference has its opposite, but the whole IS a whole. . . . And *then*,
I thought that our image of God is that if He is *All*, he has to include all this
murkier darkness and all the evil and all the grief and all the suffering and all
the victimization and crime and scapegoating and ignorance and willful pride—
all the chaotic Chaos from which God extracted light and order and sunshine, all
of heaven. I thought, "What about *that*?" and I realized that I think that God is
there, too, in all darkness, as well as in the light. God in hell. God is All. Including the dark. Including the shadow. Including hell.

I thought: God has made us to be creative like Him, to make order, to make
"earth as it is in heaven," as Jesus put it. We, too, must create; we too must extract heaven from the Chaos into which we are born. That is our meaning, our
task, and should be our *joy*.

At this point, I felt pushed to witness these thoughts in meeting. I spoke to
this effect. I concluded with the emphatic sentence: "God cannot go to hell, He
is not so All-powerful that He can alone go to hell, He *cannot* go to hell. He is
not there in hell *unless we take him there*." ("God is All")

Pauline's notion of God, and of human understanding of God, was one of
moral evolution. God could only be understood as our image of God, however imperfect. Heaven, for Pauline, was "within you"—not some objective
reality outside. Similarly, it was not important whether there was some "objective psyche" wherein there was a God with some agenda for the individual
human. Indeed, it may not even matter if "there isn't any God." Pauline
wrote, "I am inclined to think that Jung's concept of the 'collective unconscious' IS the objective Psyche."[8] The job of humanity is to make the attempt
to expound our image of God, and to orbit around that image as we are able.
Pauline wrote:

I have written elsewhere of the advancing stages of awareness that have developed in the last two millennia. . . . The final (awareness) is to perceive the . . .
dimension of incarnated reality, namely, the dark unconscious. We learn that it
is filled with the darkness of chaos, of evil, of death and destruction, of the four
horsemen of the apocalypse. We finally admit that God Himself has a dark side.
We are beginning, in large numbers to see, that the darkness *also* contains all
that undeveloped *un*aware potential light—hidden evolutionary progress. And
above all, including the whole energy and force of our *feminine* selves.[9]

Central to a seeking of God is awareness of the unconscious, and understanding that the purpose of the "ego" is that without it, without an "I," we could not know God. Our ego relates to God, but should not attempt to *be* God. That attempt, Pauline would have called sin ("I Ching"). Near the end of her life, Pauline was fond of quoting Jung to reflect her own knowledge of God: "Like Jung, I don't believe in God; I know."[10]

ON BISEXUALITY AND THE FEMININE SOUL

Upon reflection of Pauline's life and relationships in the 1930s, one cannot help but make the connection between her desire to teach and to heal and her shifting sexual material orientation, and her later understanding of the healing of the self as a bisexual self. Her own outer experience of bisexuality would mirror her later inner understanding of the bisexual nature of the self, the soul, and, on an even greater scale, of nature and the age in which we live.

At the turn of the twenty-first century, a time often referred to as the "Piscean Age," Pauline held that we were unaware of the dual nature of reality. We were unaware of the second fish swimming in balance with the first, as the piscean metaphor suggests. It is imperative, Pauline would come to understand, that the self recover not just the more celebrated masculine consciousness that recognizes materiality, but the inner, hidden feminine side, still unconscious, that recognizes spiritual meaning. The material experience and the spiritual experience are like two fish, shifting and swimming in separate directions yet desiring constant balance. Pauline's search in the 1930s for a suitable partner, as well as for radical politics and a healing profession, was an outer expression of her unconscious search for bisexuality and balance, which she would later consciously articulate. Pauline wrote of the need for bisexuality as a psychological balance:

> Actually, homosexuality versus heterosexuality should not be seen as opposites, as we usually see opposites (being in conflict). Same-sex relationship is often socially inevitable (e.g. in jail, in war, in gyn wards), fulfilling in ways not possible to heterosexuality. Same sex is bad only to those who think so, and the concept of *only* heterosexual psychology is as bad as *only* homosexual.
>
> We are all bisexual psychologically. We cannot walk on one leg. (Correspondence, "Diverse Sex," 12 January 1996)

In 1968, Pauline wrote: "It's no wonder I tend to be so ambisexual—what do I mean, 'tend'?"[11] And again in 1996, Pauline wrote the following about the "dual nature of matter": "Our total misconception of women's spirituality has always been confused with the whole shadow side of life. Our shadows enter both repressed elements a la Freud, and undeveloped, unconscious, deep, hidden dark of all yet unborn. That is, our shadows are dark—dark and simply undeveloped, potentially light darkness" ("Jungian Analysis, Renée Brand").

Pauline elaborated on the duality between female and male:

> This revolutionary concept calls for the rewriting of two histories, both the history we now have (one-sided male) and the unrealized feminine which we now begin to see as having been lived but unconsciously, and unrecognized. . . .
>
> So we go back to the initial simplicity which involves our seeing every human being of whatever sexual material orientation as psychologically bisexual. We live in a world which has repudiated the feminine principal entirely, both in men and women. The man seeks his soul in the woman and the woman seeks her own soul. Their paths differ in this development because the man has to renounce his dependence on his mother and formulate his own feminine nature in order to become a whole individual. The woman has to renounce her identity with her mother in order to become a mother herself and she has to renounce the kind of subordinate wifehood that Freud saw in favor of finding her own mate, her animus (whether flesh or spirit) within herself.
>
> Two rewrites of history. Both simplifying, both *alive*. Both Logos and loving. Neither science nor art will stand alone; neither matter nor spirit; neither truth nor love; neither creativity nor containment. Opposites are in *pairs*. Wholeness, perception, harmony, life demands them both. ("She Knew Life and Loved It")

In spite of her use of a masculine pronoun for God, Pauline saw God as Logos and loving, as male and female. In pondering the life of Mary, the mother of Jesus, Pauline concluded that reference to Mary as a virgin was reference to her "blessedness that she of all women has been chosen to be the mother of this spiritual child." Her virginity was not a reference to whether or not she had known a man. She equated Mary as the blessed one as daughter of Sophia, goddess of wisdom. The historic concept of the "exaltation of women" as bearers of blessing, of the Holy Spirit, has been evolving and just now beginning to be understood ("Virgin Birth").

The male version of God developed in the Piscean Age, over the past two thousand years. The female image has just begun to emerge and will be embraced in the coming millennium. This understanding of God and of meaning as opposition, in fact, emerged for Pauline in several further symbolic systems. The cosmic symbolic system of astrology was one of those. Indeed, notable in Pauline's Christian faith was her ability to encompass topics that often appear to other Christians to be opposite, or at least contradictory, such as Christianity and astrology. A second was a symbol that even today Pauline saw beginning to emerge in the new age as the "four-armed cross." A third dualistic metaphor was that of male and female. This metaphor, for Pauline, was intricately related to the plight of women and men in society.

Although in her middle-age Pauline was convinced women were better off married, this view was a reflection of the state of society wherein women simply did not earn as much nor have as much guaranteed stability from work. In her late eighties, Pauline wrote of the problem as a clear failure to "curtail all these chauvinistic attitudes in that they reflect on everyone's personal life as well as on our whole social structure" ("Right and Left Wing Christians"). She also saw women's lack of power not as simply a societal problem, but as a failure to develop the feminine unconscious. Pauline wrote:

> The necessity for women to speak for ourselves has always been so obvious that I didn't see it. No, the fault is not that we have failed to speak for ourselves. The problem is that we have not yet discovered our Selves; we do not know our own strength, we do not see how to contribute our own power. We can't speak for ourselves because we don't know ourselves, we tend to over-evaluate and idealize our weakness and at the same time overlook and diminish our strength. . . . Our development of the feminine as spirit is still FAR too undeveloped—because it is too unconscious.[12]

ON THE CROSS AND THE AGE OF AQUARIUS

In her last year of her life, Pauline was interviewed by Ann Kreilkamp, founder and editor of *Crone Chronicles*, for a feature in the magazine. During that interview, the two discussed the astrological significance of Pauline's life. Pauline gained new insight even at the age of ninety-five from that conversation. Kreilkamp described Pauline as a:

> . . . visionary idealist (Pisces Dun) who is driven by the need for more and deeper knowledge (Pluto in Gemini) has a natural tendency to analyze, discriminate and critique (Virgo Ascendant). The interaction of these signs feeds her quest for the wholeness and expanding perspectives on the Self (Sagittarius).[13]

Indeed, Pauline was ceaselessly on a quest for expanding perspectives of the Self. On an astrological scale, she was convinced the role of the feminine was just beginning to emerge, believing the world itself to be on the brink of a new era, a fact she celebrated. She wrote:

> The whole fourth arm of the cross is only now emerging. This Aquarian Age starts a new era. The two fish of the Piscean Age of which Jesus was the symbol have cycled two thousand times and are now replaced with the carrier of water into a new age. It is fairly tragic that we have prepared for it so badly.
> The outlook of this age is vibrant with an entire new life-attitude. As a woman, I feel particularly blessed in the knowledge that traditionally the women

have contained the water of life and the women have carried the living water from the well into the home. ("My Cross")

For Pauline, inquiry into the great mystery that is God necessarily included curiosity of events throughout time, cosmic and human. She turned to astrology to understand our moral and spiritual evolution. The Piscean Age, the past two thousand years, was characterized for Pauline by the development of temporal understanding and technology, the spiritual understanding of good and evil, and finally our emerging awareness of our knowledge. Pauline continued this line of thinking by stating that with all our technical knowledge, however, "we do not enjoy the whole life promised us in the teachings of Jesus. We have not enjoyed—and most of us have not even contemplated—the world of the unconscious the world of our Selves. This world still lies within a distant grasp for the bulk of humankind."[14] For Pauline, the coming age was one of uncovering the unconscious.

The symbol of the cross has traditionally been seen as having three arms, above ground. However, Pauline saw this traditional cross as symbolizing the masculine Trinity. Pauline came to understand the Trinitarian God, with its Father, Son and Holy Spirit imagery, as inadequately rooted. Her theology embraced a Quaternating God represented by a four-armed cross.

The fourth arm of a three-dimensional cross symbolized the rooted bottom half, buried deep into the earth. This represented the deep unconscious and decidedly feminine understanding. This image was grounded in the Earth Mother of mythology, as the one who bears human burdens.[15]

The cross was also related to another image, that of the tree, rooted deep in the earth. Pauline wrote in 1995:

So I change from the image of the cross to another common image of the Self. The Self is an anthropomorphic image. Jung had postulated that Jesus is the archetype of the Self. But as an abstract image of life, of that other tree in the garden, let us look at the tree. . . .

A tree grows upwards. You start with a little Christmas fir tree in a flower pot. You have a suitable place to plant it outdoors. Say you planted it at the birth of the child. . . . By the time the child is ready for adulthood, the tree has grown straight and tall up over the housetop. Whatever its age and height is an evolutionary matter; it will always have its trunk in heaven and its roots in earth. ("Know Thy Self")

Pauline discussed the growth of the tree outward, as well, signified by the tree rings. In this same essay, she equated these with the two fish of Pisces (her birth sign) "swimming forever in opposite directions *around* a circle." The tree rings, spiraling around the tree that is both standing in the heavens and grounded in the earth, represented life and its dualistic balance for Pauline.

Pauline's understanding of her own journey paralleled this movement from the Piscean to the Aquarian Age. Much of her life characterized conflict, mirroring the two fish of Pisces swimming eternally in opposite directions ("Paradox"). Pauline came to embrace the unconscious, the darkness and the light hidden within it, when she began Jungian analysis in middle age. She reflected, with the assistance of astrology, on the various opportunities she had experienced that had been thwarted, to "enter the darkness" in her life.

Pauline discussed the fact that Saturn, known as the "dark planet," orbits the sun and returns to the earth roughly every twenty-nine years. The first return of Saturn in Pauline's life occurred, she discovered, about twenty-nine years after her birth. In February 1934 she was "disastrously married." She recalled, "My whole way of life after that so-called marriage (turned out it was bigamous) changed for the worse. I left Teachers College without my doctorate and within the year found myself leaving my 'husband' and my job at 30 cents an hour" ("Saturn").

This first return of Saturn found her at a point where her life was drastically altered. The second return occurred in 1963, the year President Kennedy was assassinated. Pauline recalled that she was not able to "deal constructively" with her grief at his death. She had just returned from a deeply gratifying world tour, only to discover she would not be able to pursue her goal of teaching social studies as she had planned. Instead, she was to retire from teaching altogether. Once again, her life had been drastically altered at the return of Saturn, although this time, again, she did not recognize it ("Saturn").

Pauline wrote these reflections at the age of eighty-seven, the year of Saturn's third return during her lifetime. She was beginning a period of particularly intense writing at this point in 1992. Pauline saw the writing itself as a fulfillment of her vocation, finally, one that brought together her conscious and unconscious life. She wrote:

In this, your [Saturn's] last close encounter in my life, I was ready for you. . . .
I see you as introducing my last "life work and career." If I can succeed at putting into words my vision of the inner structure and order and *rightness* of that long continuum of which I am centered between Venus and Mars, love and hate, and between God and you, Saturn, between heaven and hell, facing the outer sun on one hand and the outer darkness on the other, facing life on earth on one hand and the heavenly idea on the other. If I can see the transcendent God above and His transcendent star reflected in the earth below, there is that lovely quote whose author I do not know: "The aim is to see life steady and to see it whole."
If I can get any of this on paper, get it into words, can get my symbols suffi-

ciently experienced to communicate them, then I will be entitled at the end to say, "It is finished." ("Saturn")

ON LOVE

Pauline deeply treasured her friends and loved to invite them to her home for many celebrations, especially late in her life. In 1995, for example, Pauline had a large birthday party to celebrate Pauline's ninetieth and her goddaughter Carol's fiftieth birthdays. Each year, Pauline not only sent annual Christmas and/or Epiphany letters to her friends, but most years also held an open house for any and all who could come, either on Christmas or on the day of the Three Kings. In an Epiphany invitation penned in 1997, Pauline summed up the joy of friends and of love shared:

I *have* followed the star [of Epiphany] to see beyond present human thought. But *now* I see, also, that beyond our merely human thoughts of true and false, our overly-scientific world of science and analysis, lies a whole other essential ingredient of a whole life.

Love is this equally essential ingredient. Love does not scorn our material knowledge. It does not preclude science. Nor is it an alternate viewpoint.

Spiritual knowledge is transcendent and unconquerable in that it cannot be killed, having never been born. Love *is*. . . .

She then offered an invitation to her friends:

So if you can, come to see me on January 10th—the Saturday after Tuesday, January 6th. Any time all day. Bring food if you like. . . . It will be strictly pot-lucky; the house is still a mess. But I'll order a base of Chinese food and otherwise hope for the best.

This is my annual day
on which I say,
"God bless us, every one.
I follow my star.
I'm on my way.
Whoop, whoop, hooray."
I love you and the light shines forever.
Pauline Evelyn Thompson, beginning a new life at age 92.[16]

Pauline came, in her nineties, to a place in which she could choose either to be "blissfully alone" or enriched by the presence of friends. She began one essay this way, "I didn't know 'til three-four minutes ago what I wanted to write on this blissful, empty day—wherein I hope not to speak a word to anyone

except, hopeful, my self. The door and the phone I will heed but will not in-
voke."[17]

And on Thanksgiving 1994, she chose to spend the day alone, for reflection:

> I had spent Thanksgiving Day this entirely alone by choice. I had called up the
> innumerable *persons*—living or dead, made no difference. . . .
>   On Thanksgiving Day I had many conversations with my loved ones (and
> hated ones, too) whereby I re-deemed them (in my own mind). I re-viewed them
> from Thanksgiving Day's new angle. . . . ("Paradox")

Pauline clearly experienced great love from her friends, but she understood
love expanded far beyond friends. She continued to be convinced, as a paci-
fist, that love was the essential direction for humanity. But how to get there
she was less sure, as she wrote in 1995:

> I intend to write about many aspects of loving humankind in the new age. I have
> been criticizing the old age, for the most part lovingly. But I still know practi-
> cally nothing about how to love, *how* to love. I feel that there is no possibility,
> none, of development and power and balance and joy and productivity and shar-
> ing existence with my neighbor—of life itself—without love. I have found it so
> difficult in the past, so impossible in fact to find a focus because every aspect of
> my life is involved in *how* I live it and *how* I love it. . . .

To quote my analyst of many years back: "It is better to be with love than
to be without love."[18]

Chapter Seven

Rethinking Psychology, Religion, Ethics, and Ethnography

Our evaluations of the Christian life have been so comfortable and watered down and socially useless that we have made little impact on the value systems revolving around the material world in which we live. . . .

It's a frightening and frightful responsibility to be an individual because we are each one made up out of diversities of our own unique components . . . the more we can tolerate diversity within society . . . the more adaptable we are to our individual destinies.

Pauline E. Thompson, "My Cross"

Reading Pauline Thompson's life enhances our understanding of archetypal and psychological concepts and also provides insight into issues in women's lives. This chapter is not meant to provide an exhaustive analysis of conceptual theories. Rather, posed here are musings toward teasing out meaning both in Pauline's life and in our current ideas. Understandings within psychology, religious and feminist ethics, Christianity, and ethnographic subjectivity shed new meaning and provide interesting perspectives when evaluated in light of Pauline's life.

THE INFLUENCE OF CARL JUNG

The most influential theory in Pauline's life and thought is that of Carl Jung. Although Jung's understandings of personality have undergone tremendous alterations by recent theorists, his work remains the basis of personality inventories currently used with almost popular abandon in job counseling and hiring. In such a setting, once a simple personality test is scored, individuals are often pigeonholed into one type of personality. This use of psychological theory does not allow for changes or shifting on the part of an individual. Pauline's understanding of Jung would suggest we ought to allow for such shifting.

Many of Pauline's early essays were later transferred to computer by Pauline herself, beginning in the 1980s. With that transcription came some editing. As she transcribed the writing, she altered the memory of her life. Some of the originals are lost to us. Clearly, Pauline wrote to be read. What does the life of one with such self-esteem, such a sense of "self" have to offer? Pauline herself gave one answer to this question when she wrote: "I am full of self-esteem. I admit it. I think I am not egoistic. . . ."[1] She went on to explain how in the 1990s her attitude toward the idea of the "self" changed. She came to understand she had an influence on those around her and felt it was not selfish. She believed it was her duty to be influential. She found after many years of searching that she was obligated to love everybody and to offer to others what she had of her life and thoughts. How can a person do that without self-esteem, she asked?

I asked Pauline to reflect, at the age of ninety-two, about notions of "self." She distinguished between being "self-ish" and having a "Self." Pauline agreed that the biography of a selfish woman is pointless. Recall her words from the essay "Where is My Heaven" that she was no longer tempted toward selfishness as she once was: "Used to be I wanted everything I saw, and a very restless, extroverted, tiring, tired, boring, *pointless* life it was at such times." She described the "self-ish" person as wanting everything he or she sees. A selfish person sees in others the reflection of what he or she wants or who he or she wants to be. That person then tirelessly and tiringly takes for him- or herself. A true "Self"—here we begin to recognize the influence of Jungian thought—is not like that. A true "Self" does not need to take, but understands he or she is worthy, understands his or her life is not pointless—rather it embodies meaning, whether or not he or she can see it at the time.

Indeed, Jung characterized the self as the whole personality, the "whole range of psychic phenomena" in the human. The self is only in part conscious, being made up of an interplay of light and shadow. The light is the portion of the self that is conscious, the shadow a portion of the self that is "inexperienceable" or unconscious to a person. This duality can oppose itself, the conscious self (ego) warring against the unconscious shadow. Or it can be represented as a "united duality," such as the interplay of yin and yang.[2]

Pauline inferred, as have others, that it might be possible to realize the full potential of the Self.[3] This would take a lifetime of work, work in which Pauline engaged especially throughout the second half of her lifetime.

The influence of the thought of Carl Jung on Pauline cannot be overestimated. Her thought processes could be characterized as Jungian. Images and symbols were of central importance to Pauline. To Jung, a symbol was a representation of an unknown thing (as opposed to a "sign" standing in for a known object). The tree or spiral representing growth and deeper rootedness were two of a number of symbols important to Pauline as she grew older. She was increasingly fascinated and invested in understandings of the symbolic meaning of her own life and our collective life. Astrology, stars, the existence of a grain of sand—not just its color or texture, but its significance in the world—these, as symbols, held prime significance for Pauline.

Pauline's understanding of psychological types was framed by her interpretation of Jung's thought throughout the second half of her life. According to Jung, every human has the capacity for four main functions of the unconscious: thinking, feeling, sensation, and intuition. In addition, each person is oriented by one of two attitudes toward the world, either introverted or extraverted.

Briefly, a person with an extraverted attitude is habitually energized by the external world. For one with an introverted attitude, the outside object is secondary to the subject.

These two attitudes characterize each person but are manifested in varying combinations of the function-types. "Thinking" and "feeling" are the two rational functions. For some, extraversion or introversion is manifested in thought, including the ability to know and name an object. For others, they are manifested in feeling, involving attributing value to a thing. "Sensation," or taking things in using the five senses, and "intuition," intuiting the possibilities of something, complete the pair of irrational function-types characterized by Jung.

A person has a primary mode of functioning, consisting of a pair of superior and auxiliary functions, one from the rational and one from the irrational pair. The remaining two functions are the inferior functions. Similarly either the introverted or the extraverted attitude will be superior to the other. It is possible for the inferior functions to become stronger and more integrated within a person, although in Jung's typology, a personality type does not essentially change. Andrew Samuels notes:

> Jung thought that the functions have a physiological base with a psychic component which is partially controllable by the ego. To some extent a person can choose how to operate, but the limits are probably innate. No one can dispense with any of the four functions; they are inherent to ego-consciousness. . . . But it is possible for each function to be differentiated and, within limits, integrated.[4]

These Jungian types were of primary importance to Pauline as, throughout nearly twenty years in Jungian analysis and through subsequent writings and conversations, she mused upon just what attitudes and functions formed her own personality and perceptions of herself, her world, and the greater universe.

For Jung, as for Pauline, the Self (both light and shadow) are seen as unrealized for much of life. The Self actually transcends beyond the individual self in the form of collective feelings and sensations, which Jung described as the "collective unconscious." In these can be discovered collective truths. As Pauline shifted in her faith understanding and religious orientation throughout her life, her consciousness of overriding, transcendent, collective truth deepened.

Pauline organized her autobiographical material into four categories coinciding with Carl Jung's four psychological functions. An exhibit focusing on Pauline's life at Holland Library at Washington State University chronicled her life into four parts using these categories. The first was entitled *I Am*, characterizing the years from her birth in 1905 to 1930. This period was reflective of the "sensation" function. The second phase was called *I Do* and chronicled the years 1930–1947, years characterized by the "thinking" function. The third was designated *I Perceive*, ranging from 1949–1966, years of "intuition." Finally, the years from 1960 through the 1990s were distinguished by the phrase *I Love*, indicative of the "feeling" function of Jungian theory. Pauline reacted with pleasure to the Holland exhibit, commenting it demonstrated how "a long scattered life becomes whole."[5]

Pauline saw in her life a progression and at the same time a shifting of her inner life. She lived as a genuine extravert throughout the first half of her life. Yet, by the time we met and she had reached her ninth decade, she was unquestionably a person of deep inner reflection. Hours would pass as Pauline simply sat, musing, making sense of new revelations and meaning. Jungian thought would suggest she was always an introvert, but simply made the attempt to live out of her inferior function of extraversion as a girl and young woman. Pauline believed, however, that her primary function actually shifted. At any rate, her final embracing of the inner introvert leaves us with her profound reflections to ponder.

RECONSIDERING MORAL DEVELOPMENT THEORIES

The process of "sorting through a scrap bag" of memories, as Pauline's friend Jeannie once prophetically suggested Pauline might do one day, was for Pauline a process of development as a person of religion, morality, and faith.[6] A reading of Pauline's life alongside understandings of moral and faith developmental theory not only adds insight into Pauline, but also offers new comprehension to the developmental theories themselves. Pauline's life, in interesting and surprising ways, introduces fresh insight into what it might mean to live an ethical life that spanned nearly a century. Pauline showed us a highly moral, yet feisty and fully human spirit that in many ways defies traditional understandings of ethics.

Moral theory, as developed since the 1970s, has posited a series of moral stages through which one passes as one matures, moving from a child's magical sense of the world toward universal thinking. These have been translated into stages not only of moral but also of faith development. Scotty McLennan has recently reworked the stages to demonstrate one does not just "get religion" (or not), but that religion, or faith, is a process.[7]

The process of faith development begins with a stage McLennan calls "magic." This approach to God and the world can be characterized by a child who believes Santa Claus can fly on a sleigh through the sky and enter every household on the earth in a single night. God is viewed in magical terms, as capable of anything and everything. A second stage is "reality." This occurs when, for example, a child who is now a bit older, realizes the impossibility of this magical feat on the part of Santa Claus. The person's concept of God becomes a bit more realistic, but remains childlike and naïve.

A third phase is "dependence," when a person views God neither as magical nor with just a bit more reality, but as a parent (usually a father) figure. In this stage a person bargains with God in the same way a teenager attempts to negotiate privileges and elicit promises from a parent. Pauline made such attempts, finally abandoning God for some years when she felt God unfairly closed the door for her to pursue medical school and the vocation to which she believed God had called her. It is important to note that many, if not most, adults do not progress beyond this third stage in their comprehension of God or their place in the world.

Fourth in the process of spiritual maturity is a stage of "independence," producing at times a more distant, atheistic understanding of God as one differentiates oneself from the divine presence. Pauline spent a number of years in the middle of her life as an atheist before once again embracing religion, an occurrence fostered by her introduction to Jungian psychology.

Fifth, one embraces with a kind of "second naïveté," an "interdependence" upon God. One now perceives the divine as both personal and distant, as both within and without. By now, one has abandoned any attempt to claim God can be represented solely by one particular religion or creed, seeing that the truth of the divine is both within and between and transcendent to persons—never bound by human conceptions. However, one has likely discovered a particular religious tradition in which one is rooted and in which one discovers the truth of the divine. Pauline struggled with "right-wing" understandings of Christianity as the only way to God, and with Jesus's sacrifice as a necessary atonement for sin. She rejected these exclusive notions. Yet she grounded herself in the religion of her ancestors, Christianity, in its metaphor and symbol.

The final faith stage in this process involves "unity," wherein a person is able to overcome even duality. Here, one understands God as all-encompassing being. Here the simple statement "I Am who I Am" takes on profound meaning as an overarching truth. This divine presence is experienced in all things, at all times. God is no longer something to believe in, but something that is known as permeating all of life. Toward the end of her life, Pauline did not like the idea of talking about belief in God, but rather inner knowledge of God. Pauline wrote,

> To be religious is really the same thing as saying that you have a sense of smell, or of taste, or that you can see, or digest food. To be religious means simply to have a connection, however obscure and unacknowledged, to the unseen world of the spirit. ("My Cross")

Her statement echoes undertones of the knowledge of the "being" of the divine, as stated by contemplative thinkers throughout time.[8] Pauline's understanding reflects this search for uncovering the divine in the common—a presence to which people are normally blind. This is not a faith that seeks to conjure up something that is not there, as a God in a human image. This is not a faith that believes people "call" God to them through prayer. It is one that realizes through stillness and reflection and being and action that *all* is God—that God *is*.

With such an understanding of God as all, it follows that a fully faith-filled person comprehends all humans as a part of God and hence deserving of love and compassion. Such love is not exclusively offered to those in one's own family, neighborhood, nation, race, or class. It is inclusive of persons practicing religions other than one's own. As seen particularly in her writings and her political activism, Pauline truly demonstrated a universal love for humankind. She was as quick to express love for a child needing shelter in San Francisco as for one in Bosnia. She felt it her duty to protest nuclear warfare, not because it made any immediate difference, but because she could see no alternative. Each year on Easter and Hiroshima Day, even as it became more physically painful and difficult, she joined her Quaker brothers and sisters for protests at the Livermore Nuclear Facility. Pauline did not insist people should share her view of the world (although she would not hesitate to argue her view with anyone), nor did her love stop at her own doorstep.

FEMINIST ETHICS REVIEWED

These models of moral development seem to make sense when we look at Pauline's life. Yet, when we look at feminist challenges to the six stages of moral development our characterization of Pauline becomes more complex.

It was observed in the 1980s that women were more focused on a relational human web than on detached rational principles, and more focused on caring in relationship than on universal justice. The result was that women consistently fell short on traditional scales of moral development. Women, it was thought, mature morally in different ways than men, through a three-stage process based not upon universal principles, but upon relationships. These proposed stages moved from a more selfless understanding, to a self-centered one where one becomes aware of one's own will, to a balance of concern for oneself and others. Caring for others was seen as key to virtue and moral development. Later, the role of mothering as caring was also lifted up as an empowering model of moral development for women.[9]

This formulation of women as caring was readily accepted within Western society where women have traditionally been associated with the work of caring, mothering, and a particular set of virtues set aside for women. Christian understandings of women in the traditional role of care giving had already been celebrated for centuries, promoting among women the Christian virtues of charity, selflessness, and service.

If we begin with formulations of female ethical maturity developed after male understandings of moral and faith development, coupled with traditional maternal and Christian formulations of virtue, Pauline does not fare well. Those who knew Pauline would attest to her self-absorption at times. She simply defied traditional feminine understandings of virtue. Loving, yes—but patient and slow to anger in her concern for others? No. Pauline, in many ways, fit a more masculine model moral development based upon universal stages. Pauline's life leads us to question traditional definitions of feminine virtue.

Fortunately, others have challenged these formulations as well. One question raised has been whether moral development based upon caring can be claimed to emerge uniquely from the experience of women.[10] A criticism of the development of a female ethic of care is one Pauline might have understood —that such formulations require a dualistic mode of thinking. The existence of specific "female" virtues such as patience and caring, require opposite "male" values of truth and justice, with the latter set of values seen as superior. Further, not only does such a system create a hierarchy of genders, it also requires the existence of two, and only two, opposite genders. This precludes any persons who do not fit easily within a dual-gender system. Pauline's experience and reflections upon bisexuality, for example, have no place in such a system, which normally holds heterosexuality as the only true possibility. Such a two-gender system also masks power dimensions between women. Women in privileged classes do not see that while they may care about women's rights, they care about *certain* women's rights—those of women in their own class or race. They are not necessarily championing better hours or working conditions for the women whose lives include labor that supports other women, enabling the latter to keep up their lifestyle of privilege.

Further, an ethic modeled on the "moral mother" is problematic in that the concept of "mother" itself is historically constructed. The contemporary idea of an ethic of care may simply be a reworking of eighteenth- and nineteenth-century practices of placing women on a pedestal as the bearers of morality, while robbing them of significant economic power. This places women in a position to "choose" a marginal economic position in order to be seen as virtuous.[11]

The foundations of niceness and subservience as feminine virtues, virtues that would not best describe Pauline, and notions of these virtues along with motherhood as a moral model for women, have emerged in part from Christian readings of scripture that purposely view women as subservient to men. For many years, and even recently, virtue has been equated in Christianity with being manly. Such readings exclude the positive character of women throughout Christian history and in scripture. Many Christian churches continue to privilege men with offices not open to women. Some continue to deny women's ordination by connecting Jesus's death and sacrifice with the male priesthood and apostolic succession. Additionally, the Apostle Paul's admonition "let women learn in silence with all submissiveness" continues to be used as a basis for such exclusion.[12]

The connection between a woman's ideal moral character as self-sacrifice or service using a biblical justification of male superiority over women, has been challenged in recent years. But it was first challenged over a century ago by the writers of *The Women's Bible*. Elizabeth Cady Stanton and a committee of women discussed the tradition of associating women with Eve who has been labeled by theologians as the one who introduced sin into the world, followed by the conviction that such a tendency was inherent in all women. Amusingly, several of the authors noted that in the Genesis account Eve behaved with far more courage in her pursuit of wisdom than did Adam, who was no less than "whining." The writers marveled that upon such a story men decreed their superiority over women.[13] Pauline's own words echo their humorous line of thinking:

> Women are much more complicated than men. . . . Look at the words "husband" and "wife." "Husband" meant "house-bound." There is that laughing deprecatory phrase about wives being man's "better half." If men could have committed themselves to being the yang member of a house with a yin partner with whom to share the creation of the house, well, we wouldn't have had thousands of years of patriarchy. ("Synthesis")

Stanton concluded that subservience is not a virtue among women. Rather, she declared "self-development is a higher duty than self-sacrifice" for women.[14] Pauline would agree that an ethical stance may require self-assertion and creativity, rather than either complacency or the opposite of pride, self-negation. Some have suggested that instead of being about "caring," ethics from a feminist view might better be characterized by risk-taking than by caring. Such an ethic neither seeks to control nor to be subservient, but plants possibilities for further ethical action among one's community. In this understanding of ethics, anger against social injustice is central. Pauline's experience during WWII led to her deep concern about the lack of public health in this country, a good example of an ethical stance that includes anger against an unjust social system. Pauline's experience underlines the importance of risk-taking that opens the way for others to consider ethical action against immoral structures of society.[15]

Does being ethical and honest mean being nice, or a servant? Not for Pauline. Does being ethical include integrity and honor? Indeed, these were words repeated over and over at Pauline's memorial service. Pauline embodied a strong ethic—fully human, not unnaturally gracious, feisty and angry at injustice (even at times unjustly so), yet loving and embracing beyond comprehension to those around her. At the least, Pauline's life defies feminine understandings that morality includes particularly "female" characteristics such as submission or even graciousness. At the most, Pauline's life encompasses an almost incomprehensible, universal generosity of spirit. Pauline suggests to us moral maturity does not equal perfect relationship or behavior.

RECREATING CHRISTIANITY

In the Christian tradition, delineation of the sexes and discrimination of women has been enforced with no less than the power of God. Masculinity and femininity have first been defined in strict heterosexual terms, power then granted to men, and this power reinforced when God has been defined in male terms. For many years, God the Father has functioned as the major image of the divine, particularly in Protestant Christianity and the Methodism Pauline grew up in. Mary Daly's famous quotation "if God is male, then the male is God" awakened the sensibilities of many to the potential dangers of an exclusively male image of God. The image of God becomes complicit in the continuation of patriarchy.[16]

Pauline's theological reflections include a profound reworking of a literal or even more liberal, yet orthodox, understanding of Christianity. For Pauline,

God was not an image, such as "Father." Instead, God was closer to existence, or "being." Clearly, a literal reading of the Bible or even a close devotion to creeds from church tradition missed the point for Pauline. She was interested in a deeper connection.

Pauline came increasingly to understand the mystery of timing and synchronicity in a world where God is and where all is God. Images and writings in Pauline's analysis papers and poems set alongside a rereading of Carl Jung's autobiography *Memories, Dreams and Reflections* bring a deeper understanding of synchronicity as purpose or unconscious intention.

Many persons dismiss the notion of synchronicity, define it simply as coincidence, or understand it as involving fated events. Within Christianity itself such a concept is often translated into the idea of "God's will." As represented in contemporary popular psychology, it appears little more than a secular disguise for this Christian idea. Often, understanding an event to be God's will allows one to relinquish responsibility. After all, if one can rationalize how events fit with one another, then those events must have been *supposed* to happen that way. Hence, one is absolved of sin or of wrestling with the existence of any evil that may have brought about the events. Pauline did not understand synchronicity as an event ordained by God that relieved one of accountability. Pauline understood both synchronicity and the being of God as embodying meaning, myth, and paradox.

Seventeen years of analysis brought Pauline into a pattern of dream analysis and reflection toward the discovery of the unconscious that enabled her to make meaning out of her entire life. She came to understand, as Carl Jung wrote that, "life is—or has—meaning and meaninglessness. I cherish the anxious hope that meaning will preponderate and win the battle."[17] Pauline learned to embrace the fool and the wise woman, the shadow and the ego, and the slowly emerging yet still largely unconscious connections between them.

Pauline wrote of her analysis and active imagination drawings:

My Jungian Analysis began in October 1949 and with intervening breaks ran to mid-1966. My imagination became increasingly active but the pictorial output was the most extensive at the beginning.

I used several media. The paper was always accidental; one of my most beautiful products was on a paper towel.

The most meaningful and important was done in Easter week of 1952. At that time, I showed a detailed picture which included myself kneeling near a crossroad with a well including the rope and bucket nearby and two sparrows in the sky reflected in the water below. Easter *1992* without any memory whatsoever of the 1952 painting I wrote a paper entitled, "My Four Stars.". . .

My ability as a painter fully demonstrates the value of active imagination regardless of total inability as an artist. Out of this whole album, this one painting is worth *all* the rest. It tells me unmistakably that one can be, that I was, on my journey all my life, conscious or no. It reminds me of Jung's stone-carved portal saying that God is there whether one knows it or not. I share it because I want to affirm as publicly as possible the value of one's past as the foundation of one's present.[18]

Pauline's Christian theology challenged creedal and literal understandings and moved toward a deeper knowledge. She rejected the traditional image of the godhead as the Trinity, and embraced a "Quarternating God." This encompassed the feminine element abandoned by the masculine Trinity and balanced the male God with the female, while embracing a rootedness in the earth as a balance to upward transcendence.

Pauline also challenged traditional understandings of Christ's atonement on the cross. She did not see it as an opportunity for absolution of sin, thus allowing people to avoid further responsibility. She was not alone in intuiting that any glorification of Christ on the cross as necessary for human salvation can amount to little more than a celebration of male violence.[19] The point of Jesus on the cross was to triumph over death, not to glorify a violent death, which countless more humans have suffered in innumerable ways. She emphasized Jesus's death on the cross not as the ultimate in human suffering, but as a triumph over injustice. Pauline perceived Jesus's life was an invitation to love all of humanity. His life was one centered in the constant knowledge and reality of an ever present God.

As a believer, Pauline might be characterized by the term gnostic, as defined by Elaine Pagels: "Insofar as *gnostic* refers to one who 'knows,' that is, who seeks experiential insight. . . ."[20] Pauline's knowledge of God's presence and her embracing of the experience and tradition of Quaker silence and community reflect a rare gnosis found within Christianity.

ANALYZING SUBJECTIVITY AND REFLEXIVITY IN RESEARCH

At Pauline's memorial service I encountered dozens of people whose lives were transformed by her. Similarly Liza Rognes, who catalogued some of Pauline's papers in the archives of Holland Library at Washington State University, affirmed the transformative influence Pauline had on a person. When working on Pauline's papers and finding countless pieces missing or out of order, Liza at times grew extremely frustrated (as did many of us at points when dealing with her papers). But, Liza reflected, "I realize now how Pauline has changed my life—more than anyone in a number of years—as a result of my own becoming so involved in *her* life."[21]

What does it mean to collect and write a life history, yet at the same time to be transformed by that history? Anthropologists have long debated whether an ethnographic approach, which I took in gathering this life history of Pauline, can be carried out objectively.[22] It is important for a researcher to look reflexively upon her or his own race, class, and gendered position in relation to that of the subject. Such a politics of representation is addressed by the practice of reflexive anthropology and includes deconstructing power relations in language and culture.[23]

Working with Pauline's life brought another layer to bear upon ethnographic research—the acknowledgement of the moral agency of a subject in the writing of her life.[24] Even when a researcher acknowledges power relations, it is still possible to falsely essentialize a subject as representative of a group (such as a group of "elder Americans") thus erasing the moral agency of the subject herself. Pauline would not allow such erasure.

Pauline's own influence in this project was obvious from the start. The seed for this work lay in an autobiography begun by Pauline in 1979, which developed into well over a thousand pages and was eventually included in the papers she offered to the WSU Manuscripts, Archives and Special Collections.[25] As Pauline herself earlier reflected upon how to write her autobiography, she wrote in her essay "My Four Stars": "My original ideal of trying to choose the best highlights out of my long, tempestuous, varied careers seems unimportant and irrelevant to the spiritual personality who is so rapidly crystallizing from them."

As I attempted to capture this emergent spiritual personality, Pauline's written work and input became central to my work. For example, the candidness of our conversation became a player in this process. Initially I was warned that when I went to interview Pauline I would be lucky to get answers to my questions. It was reported to me that she would look away, be silent, or change the subject when she did not wish to answer. In subsequent conversations with Pauline, my experience proved the complete opposite. At one point, for example, aware that other researchers never quite got straight the nature of Pauline's relationships, I asked her about her sexual history. She immediately went to a pile of papers, rummaged through, and produced a list she once compiled of every individual she had slept with in her life.

Pauline's active participation in this process was key in this unfolding ethnographic process. Indeed, I came to see her silences as indications that she was deeply pondering, and I learned that in time she often revealed to me a deeper meaning implied in one of my questions than I myself had considered. At one point I was curious, for instance, after looking through her work in the WSU Archives, about the fact that Pauline religiously saved copies of her side of correspondence but not nearly so regularly letters sent to her. Af-

ter my first few intensive days interviewing her, I asked where were the letters *from* Wilbur, the long-distance lover she wrote to copiously in the 1930s.
She paused a very long time, then admitted I had hit upon a very insightful
question—one that led her to a new insight. She replied, practically, that she
believed she had them and had simply not offered them for some reason with
the other papers she gave the WSU libraries. Perhaps they were misplaced, or
she had intended to copy them before giving them away. Pauline noted at that
point that she wanted to ponder my question overnight, and we could talk
some in the morning. The next day, Pauline commented that what I thought
was a simple question prompted her to discover a new way to *think*. It is not
enough to "just say no." One has to say "what will I do, instead?" Indeed, we
need to be connected. It is not enough to just reflect our own feelings, our
own acceptance or rejection of another. We must pay attention to their response as well. As a lifelong learner, we must ask "what next?" How did
Wilbur respond to her letters? It was a question loaded with insight.[26]

Not only were Pauline's moral agency and active participation in this
process central to the writing of this life history, but her complex theology of
the existence of God, her compassion for the world, her anger and human-
ness, her vast love, and her unquestioning knowledge of the truth of synchronicity in life influenced my understandings. According to Pauline's
views, Christian morality is not just about outer, individual behavior. At a
deeper level, morality encompasses compassion for all of humanity. It is
about understanding our complicity in societal structures of sin. It is about
love, rather than exclusion. And morality is about integrity more than pleas-
ing others. Pauline's long life and words offer permission to mature and age
into passion and conviction without needing the approval of others. Pauline's
gnosis points toward a deep experiential understanding of Christianity morality. Her experience demonstrates a lacing of synchronicity in life of which
many are unaware.

Following my first interviews with Pauline, I recorded the following:

> She sits not like a ninety-two year old who has recently broken her neck, but like
> a teenager. When Pauline Thompson leans back on her couch, only her neck
> reaches the backrest (the back cushions have been removed as she sometimes
> sleeps there). She sits with her head bent forward, one foot upon the sofa, one
> upon the floor. She sometimes suddenly sits up straight, silent, her eyes looking
> off to the side as though she sees some new wit or wisdom, before beginning to
> speak again.
>
> I have now spent two full days and one evening (why does it seem much
> longer?) with Pauline . . . throughout the time listening . . . can one listen "pas-
> sionately"? I sit so attentively that my dinner often grows cold (as does Pauline's
> while she talks), knowing that the place I am in is a place of honor, somehow.

Did Moses feel foolish when asked to remove his shoes in front of a burning bush? I have the feeling that in recent years many persons have sat before Pauline, kicked their shoes off, and felt a bit foolish—yet with an inner knowledge they were witnessing a sacred moment or hour or day before her.

How does one describe Pauline? I do not dread aging and acquiring more creases in my face when I watch her. Every line seems to tell a story, as she truly believes every line on her hands, each of them, do. I was here a few hours before I saw her face wrinkle up into a smile, then that marvelous smile and its accompanying giggle came more and more frequently. But her eyes—a light blue-grey—it is as if I can see right into them. They do let a person into the soul, a very complicated soul at that.[27]

The experience of synchronicity—that of revelations from seemingly unrelated events intertwining unexpectedly—became increasingly important to Pauline, as did her understanding of symbols. As I read and mused upon her life, I too experienced synchronistic moments, as have others in connection with Pauline.

For example as I began to study her life, the biblical image of the burning bush occurred to me as I sat spellbound before her. I also pictured the images of a daisy or tree rings. Pauline usually began at the center, moved off on a tangent as if to outline a petal, returned to the center, and moved off toward the periphery again. Only after imagining those images myself did I discover her quotes regarding the tree representing her revelations uncoiling like a spiral, and her own drawings that could have been created with the use of a Spirograph (had she had one). Her active imagination drawings included images one might expect such as houses, faceless persons, and phallic symbols. One seemingly unremarkable flower outline, however, mirrored an image I had already conceived of her life. Appearing like a mandala, the flower was repeated throughout Pauline's drawings spanning fifty years. It was often eight-petaled, and the petals resembled those of a poinsettia, contained within a circle. The flower was at times colored bright reds, blues and yellows, or alternatively pastels.[28]

In 1993, Pauline wrote:

We humans are prone to philosophize about what it is that makes us human in addition to being animal. I am coming to believe that perhaps our ability to remember is the distinguishing quality of being human. I mean, the ability to remember abstractions, to make images . . . to remember in such a way that the images can be added or subtracted or altered—and that consequently future behavior can be altered also—that is what it is to be human. . . .

I am so grateful to God for my memory. It enables me to live my life over and over again without having to start each day green and new and insecure. My memory has made a mountain out of my past, and each day the mountain gets higher and the perspective gets wider and I can experience today fully because I have learned to experience yesterday fully.

And so at last I also know that tomorrow I shall experience fully, too. I shall soon be going out the one and only door with a full backpack of memories. (I recognize that I may go out the door before my body does but that's no matter. What I have just said is true and I am grateful to God that it is so).

My griefs are for the world—world sorrow, world grief. Jesus was a happy man, although He was also known as the Man of Sorrows. He was sorry for his brothers and sisters, for us children, just as I have expressed grief for modern children. But my personal memories are of redemption and joy. They bring about the changes that are development and positive growth.[29]

Pauline's memories, developmental growth, and moral agency were integral —almost participants themselves in the writing of this life history. My experience of the moral force and importance of Pauline's life and character echoed that of others who knew her and was captured by Pauline in her own writings. Pauline herself gave us a hint about what we might gain from knowing her:

I have gradually come out of so many causes—and society as a whole has come out of so many causes! "Let it all hang out" was a trite saying twenty years ago. We had all perhaps been much wiser to have stayed in some of them. But my instincts have changed. Instead of secrecy, the opposite need has arisen. It is not enough to have to come out of this closet. . . . I don't need just to expose my secret; I need to *betray* it. I need to *tell*. I want you to know.

Once before, against my own instincts, I tried to share my [deepest] . . . experience with a loved relative. . . . I thought I told it well, but when I finished she waited for me to go on and finally asked, "Is that all?" So I hesitate to introduce myself to you, except that I feel I can never reveal anything of who I really am unless I do. To tell about myself is to acknowledge and exert the precious, unappreciated, often unrecognized, almost boundless freedom of old age. If I tell you and you don't understand or value—no matter; if you do understand and value, I have been able to give you something before I die, and I am the happier for trying to share.[30]

Pauline learned there was value in accepting ambiguity and uncertainty which in time become clearer. Although Pauline was often extremely impatient, her writings revealed she understood the significance of life as a process. Pauline wrote "It is as if I had been stumbling and falling all my life, consciously off-course, without even knowing there was a course" ("My Stars! My Journey"). When late in her life she recalled childhood memories whose significance she did not recognize until after age eighty-seven, she acknowledged "And it is ok that I didn't know until now" ("Four Stars").

This ethnographic process reflects Pauline's understanding that as a life grows longer and reflection upon that life deeper, and as more information is gathered, the interactive process widens the perspective of both researcher and subject.

Figure 4. Symbolism Drawing, Active Imagination Drawings by Pauline E. Thompson, December 1964

Conclusion

Request

God, give me a life like a Persian shawl,
Not years like stacks of cold white sheets,
Life fashioned richly in intricate pattern,
Not days unspotted and faultlessly blank.

Put in silver and gray and touches of scarlet.
Let there be splashes of deep, purple pain,
But save me, oh God, from righteous aloofness
And the barren bleached web of its loom.

Let the white threads there are be of seaspray
And scattering of wild plum blossoms.
Here gleam the delight of a baby's sweet body,
There the piled clouds of early September.

Out of the fabric with masterful plan
Let the gold glimmer through that is moonlight
And woodthrush song, a sip of champagne,
The breast of one woman who loved me.

And let there be lost in the blending
With the deathless blue of seven rare handclasps,
The eyes of my lover, a turquoise I lost,
The deep fairy blue of violin music.

Outline some motifs in keen black hate,
Weave in the crimson thread of desire
On a somber woof of the ache in waiting
For one I hourly pray will return.

And so when the weaving is ending
And I might sit with taut folded hands,
Absorbed in the goodness of nothing,
My mouth a hard orthodox line,
I shall trace with a pale withered finger
The colorful maze of my years.
Wistfully smile through remembering mists.
Then when the shuttles are stilled at last,
I'll gather my fare folds about me and . . . go.

Margaret L. Truesdale, Washington State College, 1928

Pauline wrote, "The *journey* is the thing."[1] Throughout her life's journey, Pauline earned several nicknames. One of her early nicknames was "Hard-Way Thompson," a name she felt was well-deserved. Before that, however, she earned the title, "Slow Reaction-Time Thompson." Pauline believed this, too, was true. She wrote:

My friend Jeannie said to me many years ago, "Pauline, you are a very hard person to live with. You go racing around throwing bits of life into your scrap bag, never properly looking at them. But I think you will make a very nice old lady, if you should live so long. Then maybe you will take the things out of your scrap bags and look them over and make them into something." ("Letter to Friends")

In her eighties and nineties, Pauline opened up the "scrap bag" of her life and sorted through it, stating that finally "a long scattered life becomes whole" (P.E.T Exhibit). By her midnineties, she was able to say that although her body failed her, she had never been more alive in spirit, more able to awaken each day and wonder what joys or troubles the day would bring, more clear in her knowledge of God. In 1996 Pauline wrote of the depth of her contentment and her conviction as a sentient, elder human being:

I am personally deeply, *deeply* content in my certainty that I am a soul, part of a meaningful immortality and related both to God on the one hand and my fellow creatures on the other. I personally have been blessed far beyond the average creature and very far beyond my own deserts. I am happy in the way the 23rd Psalm describes happiness.

But as a social animal, I find myself sad and frustrated and inadequate and just downright angry. I think I can negotiate with anybody who is willing to negotiate. Anybody. But I haven't the foggiest how to deal with people who *want* to be my enemy and who *want* me to know that they have the power and I might as well shut up and fade away.

I thought to stop here. I thought I was through. I have vented my anger ("vent" is another interesting word in this context), but I do have a final word

beyond the anger. It relates to the obvious fact that in addition to the world col-
lapse (and possibly good riddance), there is an even greater certainty that eventually we ourselves are the answer to the question of "Why not now?" Eventually truth—and love and harmony—will prevail. If I can get more insight, I will
tell it. I intend to work at it. But I do not need to be angry with myself because
I can't make them listen and I do not need to be angry at them because they
won't listen. We come and go like mayflies but our souls have always been and
always will be. . . .

   So for me the paths of peace have become too civil and too passive. So I will
not be too very self-critical. I have tried. I have succeeded in achieving a more
forward-looking stance. I will quiet my uproars. But I shall also look for a different drummer. And if I can't find a different drummer to my liking, why, then,
I guess I shall have to take up drumming.[2]

There is little doubt that Pauline Thompson followed a different drummer,
and that she was herself a drummer. As her goddaughter Carol stated at
Pauline's memorial service, Pauline didn't just take up drumming, she made
the drum! Embedded in her life was a truth—that to be a human being is not
to be without anger or idiosyncrasies. It is to be sentient, to be searching, to
make meaning, not as follower, but—to borrow a phrase from Tillie Olsen—
moving to a "rhythm of one's own." Toward the end of her life she could vow
similarly to Olsen's words, to be "able to live within". . . knowing "somewhere an older power that beat for life. Somewhere coherence, transport,
meaning."[3]

   In 1994, Pauline reflected that she had lived "the richness of a whole life
as a 20th century woman, educated, traveled, generally well-fed and clothed
and sheltered, and *loving* and *loved*. What more could one ask? I have been
at the foot of the cross; I was at the door of the tomb; I have had my vision
and my promise of heaven; I have glimpsed it whole; I am content."[4]

SECURING A LEGACY

Pauline was far from consistently content throughout her final years and
months, however. She became increasingly concerned with where and how to
leave her material possessions upon her death. They included some savings
and her home, the latter valued multiple times what she had paid for it in
1967. In the early 1990s, she was in touch with people from her first alma
mater, Washington State University. Through a series of visits to WSU and
discussions with the libraries, the College of Education, Women's Studies,
and the WSU Foundation office, Pauline determined to leave her home and
her papers to WSU. She donated her writings to Holland Library at WSU,

along with a monetary gift for the work of cataloging. In 1994 Sarah Barber-Braun and members of the library and archival staff put together a display including papers and photographs from the wagon train that carried her ancestors to Walla Walla, Washington, to later work of Pauline.

At the same time, in April of 1994, Pauline was awarded the first WSU Women's Studies Distinguished Alumnus Award, and visited WSU to receive the award. Conversations with the Director of Women's Studies, Jo Hockenhull, led to the organization of a course Pauline would offer through Women's Studies the coming fall. Pauline lived in Pullman for the duration of the course, which was entitled "Women and the Jungian Feminine." The undergraduate students who took the course were at times puzzled by, and at others enthralled by Professor Thompson, each one encouraged by her to gain insight through doing a great deal of personal writing.

In addition to WSU, many others "discovered" Pauline in the last decade of her life.[5] While much attention centered on Pauline's character and interviews, Pauline's own late life project centered around her own writings and memoirs, in many ways her surrogate children. Throughout her life she wrote profusely, but rarely had her work been published, although she would have liked to see it in print.

As Pauline herself said several times, one could not understand her current position unless one heard her entire story and what a "fool" she was. Part of her foolishness was her lack of follow-through with her writings. Pauline sought meaning, and each writing led to a new idea to which she immediately turned. While Pauline's vocations varied from educator to nurse to psychologist to writer, it was this latter vocation that Pauline seemed to believe would bring her a final peace with her life's work. Recall Pauline's reflection upon the return of Saturn at age eighty-seven: "If I can see the transcendent God above and His transcendent star reflected in the earth below. . . . If I can get any of this on paper, get it into words, can get my symbols sufficiently experienced to communicate them, then I will be entitled at the end to say, 'It is finished.'" ("Saturn")

Parabola Magazine was interested in the life and writings of Pauline, and Pauline embarked upon an ambitious trip in the fall of 2000 to New York to attend a film festival sponsored by *Parabola*. According to those closest to her, Pauline seemed to know this was to be her last trip. During her travels, Pauline had the opportunity to visit Bellevue Hospital where she had worked as a nurse many years before, and to see Greenwich Village and the home where she had lived. It was a time of remembering. Along with the memories came fear that she might not be remembered. Pauline focused on securing a future for her memoirs, believing they would be the legacy she left to the world. Worn out from her visits and her wish to know such a legacy would be taken care of, Pauline ate little during the trip.

REFLECTIONS ON A JOURNEY

By the time Pauline returned to her home in San Francisco she was weak with a virus. Friends who visited her soon recognized her deteriorating health and took her to the hospital. After a brief stay, she was taken to a nursing home. Worried by Pauline's continued refusal to eat, her friend Kay Anderson organized eight friends from the San Francisco Society of Friends to take turns sitting with Pauline at mealtimes, to answer her phone, and otherwise assist her.

"We were there to accompany her on her final journey," Kay later reflected. "And that's really what we did—accompany her."[6] Pauline was extremely agitated in those final weeks of her life, not used to relinquishing control, yet unable to care for herself. This agitation continued into a final week, when it was determined that Pauline would return home with twenty-four-hour nursing care, as was her wish.

While in the nursing home, friends report it was difficult to talk with Pauline. The phone rang, visitors came, and Pauline was often less than gracious upon their arrival. One friend recalls walking out of Pauline's room to find a dozen beautiful flower arrangements all for Pauline. The staff responded that Pauline refused to have them in her room, stating unequivocally, "I'm not dead yet!" In Jungian terms, Pauline may have been little concerned with the sensate pleasure from her surroundings. Pauline was clearly, however, an intuitive thinker, a fact we have glimpsed in the memoirs quoted throughout this life history, and wove meaning out of seemingly mundane events into an intricate pattern.

As she reflected upon her life in the few years that preceded her death, Pauline wove meaning into the various stages of her life. She divided those into stages symbolized by her image of four stars. The transcendent. The reflected. The fool. The Self. Relating each to Jungian functions, as Pauline associated them throughout her life, these four stars complete a picture of a life deeply lived.

The *transcendent* star. Pauline first saw the star from her bedside as a girl, when she was, she felt, experiencing the world through "sensation." Bodily perception and physical change characterized her years in Spokane and Colville with her mother and father, grandmother, aunt and brother. Her belief in the world contained a sense of magic.

In a poem entitled "Silence," Pauline recalled her childhood, a magical time when she believed what she heard followed by the years when that naïve faith began to die:

> "Are you there?" Or even just "*Are* you?"
> Is there any Thing to respond? Anything?
> In childhood days I had had faith, so of course I heard answers.
> I heard voices as Joan of Arc heard her voices.
> Out of the silence.
> If you have faith, you have faith.
> Just like that.
> And you hear.
> But if faith dies, you don't have faith.
> And you don't hear.
> That is what we call "dead silence," instead.
> It's that simple and that soundless.
> The louder the cry, the louder and emptier and longer the ensuing silence.[7]

For many years Pauline lived in a second functioning state of "thinking." Her faith understanding was one of reality, slowly turning into dependence upon reasoning and thinking. She moved into a state of *reflection*, seeing the second star as a reflected star. She completed the first phase of her education, then struck out independently to the east to further pursue her quest for knowledge.

By the time Pauline reached her fifties she discovered a third function deep within—that of "intuition." She continued in "Silence":

> *God's Answer*
> Then, after long turbid years, there was an answer.
> It was a star, and it came from a star, and it came about a star, and it was the
>   light of the world.
> And it, too, shone in silence.
>
> And both silences were full of awe.
> First had been the empty silence following the unanswered question:
>   Is there a God?
> Second, came the full unanswerable immeasurable silence following the answer.
> The Bible says God spoke out of the whirlwind, and what is more silent than
>   the air settling after a whirlwind has tortured it and then dropped it?

The poem continues by making connections between silence and losing her virginity, "perhaps the worst silence of my becoming." Pauline recalled what a "fool" she was in any intimate relationships she formed. The star of the *fool*, of Aldebaron, emerged as she saw how she allowed herself to be manipulated and to manipulate. She grew into a faith that was both independent and inter-dependent upon a mysterious God.

Finally, following the silencing she experienced in relationships, Pauline discovered deep "feeling," just knowing the silent presence of God. This is the emergence of the star of the *Self*. Pauline continued:

> *Answers from the Silence of Hell*
> But there finally came the answer. Yes.
> God spoke.
> I can't say how it was that He spoke silently, but he did.
> I dreamed one silent word. Not a voice. Not in print.
> Just *there*. A being word
> I found it called to me *by name* and said, "I am Here. I am responsive. I dwell in you in depth but accessible to consciousness. . . ."
> God is the silence of being. . . .

Silence reflects Pauline's maturing knowledge that it is all along the self that blocks the transcendent from being reflected in a pool below. She came, in the end, to see the unifying truth of love for all people. She came to embrace a larger Self, enabling her to glimpse the illumination of transcendent love, of the silence of God's being.

THREE FINAL STORIES

Three final stories illustrate the triumph of love in Pauline's life.

Outside, on a windy winter San Francisco afternoon in January 2001, two homeless men sat leaning against the front door, the smells of restaurant food, dusty wind and urine filled the air, as crushed paper cups blew along the sidewalk and taxis zoomed through the streets. Inside the Society of Friends House, lines of chairs four rows deep were set up to form a square, as though pulled up around a table, surrounding an empty square of pinkish brown carpet. The room was simple, unadorned, windowless except for the skylight overhead. Nearly all the chairs were occupied by the large, silent crowd gathered for Pauline Thompson's memorial service. Two front rows were reserved for Carol Brownson and her family, Pauline's "family."

There was silence. The Quaker service had begun.

An elderly man shifted and scratched his knee. A petite woman in her sixties, who sat with Pauline frequently during her final days, pulled out a handkerchief. A striking, tall, young, blond woman, whose education in England Pauline had generously supported, wept silently. Three rows back, several men in business suits shifted uncomfortably in the silence. In front of them a young woman's face bore a worried look — pain, even — at recent memories of experience many shared with her of this woman whose tongue could belittle one in seconds.

Slowly people took turns, rising to speak. An African American man told of feeling instantly welcomed at his first Quaker meeting when Pauline's blue eyes gazed at him across the floor of a Sunday Friends Meeting. A young white woman told of going to Pauline's home to assist her with her garden, next being asked to come inside and help clean out a clothes closet, only to find herself sitting with Pauline, reminiscing for hours about the days when she wore each item of clothing (and subsequently putting them all back into the closet). Friends testified of fifty years of drinking tea and hearing remarkable stories spun out of the most ordinary events. The words "integrity," "stimulation," and "love" were repeated many times as stories of Pauline's philosophizing were recounted.

There was genuine laughter upon hearing the words of one friend commenting that he knew Pauline would let God know if God did not behave. Accounts were told of Pauline kneeling for arrest before guards in riot gear at Livermore Nuclear Facility, friends swearing that with her flair for drama, she winked as she kneeled in the hope that the press was nearby.

After a brief silence, Pauline's friend Kay Anderson stood and related three stories. She began by recalling a scene after Pauline had broken her neck from a fall down the stairs. It was many months before Pauline was properly diagnosed. She was thought to be exaggerating her pain, and Pauline grew outraged at her treatment by the medical establishment at the time. Following a proper diagnosis, the Society of Friends held a meeting in which they prayed for Pauline's healing. Kay recalls she had just learned that morning of Pauline's condition, and was very concerned that she would be disabled permanently as a result. The Friends gathered in meeting and "put her in the light" — holding a strong image of Pauline in her bed before them in silence, imagining a cone of light surrounding her.

As Pauline was held in prayer, another Friend, Sue, requested prayers for her husband Tom's grant that would enable him to work on transportation for the handicapped in Russia. The grant was at that moment in the hands of Washington officials. Immediately Kay's vision broadened to include a group of four or five men and women in grey suits sitting in chairs and shuffling papers around Pauline's bed. Kay recalled "the image was so incongruous, I almost laughed out loud." She later reported that from that moment on she had no doubt that the money would be forthcoming, for Pauline would convince those bureaucrats of its importance. The money would be received, Kay was sure, but she was unconvinced Pauline would recover from the broken neck. Kay stood in a Quaker meeting and shared her vision and gratefulness that her prayers were answered when she later learned Tom had received the funds. And Pauline's broken neck healed.

A second story. Kay arrived at the nursing home at lunchtime during the final weeks of Pauline's life. She took Pauline's hand and asked her if she would be willing to join Kay in a "meeting for worship," a time of silent prayer. At first Pauline protested, saying she was in no shape to go to the Quaker House just now. Kay insisted she meant right here and now. Pauline was reluctant, but Kay assured her she could stop when she wanted to.

Pauline took Kay's other hand in her own. They sat together for five or ten minutes in complete silence—Pauline in her bed, Kay sitting beside it. When the time had elapsed, Pauline suddenly opened her eyes and said, "That was one of the deepest meetings I have ever experienced." And she reported on the meeting to other friends who came by in subsequent visits.

Finally, Kay reported the story of Pauline's final moments alive. On Thursday morning, November 30, 2000, Pauline asked her nurse (whom she had treated less than kindly) to bring her something for her the pain in her foot. Her nurse returned and cared for Pauline's foot. Pauline then took the nurse's hand, kissed it, and said "I love you." And she died.

A longtime friend of Pauline's, who along with other friends Pauline wanted little to do with during her last weeks of life, said that when she heard of Pauline's final words they made everything alright. Pauline's friend reflected, "That she took the hand of a perfect stranger and said 'I love you'— I took it that was for me."

As Pauline wrote in her preface at age ninety-four, "I *know* now in a new way . . . and more deeply still—even if it proves to be unsuccessful—that 'Love is the answer.'"

Notes

PREFACE

1. Pauline said Lincoln Steffens defined "successful failure" as the positive reversal of unsuccessful failure. In this preface she went to explain "Steffens' example of an unsuccessful failure was President Wilson's evaluation of the Treaty at Versailles as the best we could have achieved 'under the circumstances,' instead of saying that with this Treaty we are creating World War II."

Pauline typed out this preface upon reading a 1999 draft of this book just a year and a half before her death in November 2000 (Author's files). After typing her preface, she apparently spent some time reviewing it. In a manner typical of Pauline's writings, the copy she finally sent me was heavily edited with phrases scratched out and lengthy scribbled notes in the columns. The typed copy was initially written as a preface, referring to me in third person. She then scratched out references to "Gail" and changed them to "you" in letter form. I have retained the third person references here.

INTRODUCTION

1. "My Stars! My Journey," 8 January 1993, Pauline E. Thompson Papers, Cage 676, Manuscripts, Archives, and Special Collections, Holland Library, Washington State University, Pullman, Washington (hereafter cited as Thompson MSS). The first time a document from the Thompson MSS is cited here, it will appear in a note; subsequent references to the same document will appear by title in parenthesis in the text.

2. "God is All," 10 September 1993, Thompson MSS.

CHAPTER ONE

1. The paradox of Pauline is illustrated by her reaction to a sketch drawn of her in 1985 (see Figure 1). She wrote in her album it was "most unflattering," yet she kept the sketch which reveals her character well. Many very flattering and stunning photos were taken of her throughout her younger years by her friend and photographer Erna Bert Nelson. Available in Thompson MSS.

2. Pauline's version of her contribution to Friends House included the belief that she gave the former, a pivotal founding gift, but according to the manager of Friends, it amounted to the latter, a down payment for her own residence there. Pauline's connection with the Friends brought her many of her most treasured friendships in later life. The poem beginning this chapter was written by a friend of Pauline's from the San Francisco Society of Friends, Jeanne Lohmann. It first appeared in a newsletter of the San Francisco Religious Society of Friends, 1983, and can be found in "Sex/Gender, 'Pauline's Story,'" n.d., Thompson MSS.

3. Friends House Directory page on Dr. Pauline E. Thompson, Author Interview, May 1997.

4. Author Interview, November, 1997.

5. Archived in Thompson MSS.

6. Louisa J. Estes, 1862, "Reminiscences of her Trip Across the Plains," Thompson MSS. Estes places the start of the journey in May of 1862, others say March or April. Another source chronicling the experience of the Kennedy train's trek and their arrival at the massacre at American Falls is found in the diary of Hamilton Scott with notes from Alvin Zaring, published as a series in the *Power County Press*, American Falls, ID, 7 July through 4 August 1949. Featured with the first installment is an article on E. E. Zaring, a relative of Pauline's maternal grandmother, who was the only living survivor of the Massacre Rocks incident. Another diary of the trek is the Jane A. Gould Journal, published by the Friends of Massacre Rocks, 1986.

7. *Walla Walla Statesman*, 8 February 1867, 3.

8. For a thorough geneology of the Paul and Zaring families, see "Maternal Genealogy Charts" Compiled by Jim Hockenhull, 1995, and "Paternal Genealogy Charts" Compiled by Jim Hockenhull, 1995, Thompson MSS. Many additional genealogy charts, photographs, and memoirs of Pauline's family gathered by Pauline may also be found in Thompson MSS.

9. "Childhood," 11 November 1993, Thompson MSS.

10. Dreams and Associations, April–July 1950, Thompson MSS. The first time a folder listed under the Thompson MSS series "Dreams and Associations" containing journal entries from a specific year is cited, it will appear in a note; subsequent entries from the same folder will appear as Dreams followed by a date in the text.

11. Rex became a film representative, selling film rentals to movie houses near Bremerton. He secretly married Clara Griggs so his wife could teach, but when she became pregnant, she lost her teaching job. Rex worked in Port Orchard where he bought a theater. However, a strike ruined theater business, and Rex was forced to rent out the theater. Pauline submits some Thompson family theaters were run by Rex's

family. She perceived him as a mover and a shaker as mayor and business owner in his town. He had two sons, who both served in the military during World War II.

12. "Father and Me," 20 October 1978, revised 1993, Thompson MSS.

13. "My Stars! My Journey." The story is Annie Fellows Johnston, *The Little Colonel's Chum: Mary Ware* (Boston: L.C. Page & Co., 1908).

14. "Four Stars," 21 February 1992, Thompson MSS.

15. I came to understand this point of view held by Pauline when I received a call inviting me to a job interview while in the midst of an interview I was conducting with Pauline. I decided to ask Pauline's advice on a question the pending interview posed in my mind. I told her I might be offered a professionally advancing, but more time consuming, position with another university. My question to Pauline was whether it really mattered in the long run which job I chose at that particular moment in my life. After a characteristic pause in which Pauline pondered the question, she finally looked up and said that for me, it did not matter. Instead, what mattered was how I lived my soul journey.

16. See the essay entitled "My Color Red," in which Pauline discussed her personal unconscious as symbolized by the color red, 14 December 1991, Thompson MSS.

17. Commonly called Washington State College or WSC, the official name of the college was State College of Washington, and is now Washington State University.

18. "Virgin Birth," 30 December 1992, Thompson MSS.

CHAPTER TWO

1. "Bertha Myself," 2 June 1992, Thompson MSS. Pauline went through a number of revisions of this essay, all of which can be found in Thompson MSS.

2. "My Philosophy, 'Not a Bad Hand for a Physician,'" 1951, Thompson MSS.

3. Margaret married Vernon M. Gibbs in 1928. Their daughter Carol Brownson became Pauline's goddaughter and eventually executor of Pauline's estate. Margaret would marry again to Richmond Montague in 1951. She wrote the poem "I Have No Time" (see Chapter 3) in 1927. Pauline quoted the poem in a letter to friends in Correspondence of Pauline E. Thompson, July–December 1941, Thompson MSS.

4. "Hal Richardson, Memorabilia," Thompson MSS.

5. See Peter F. Carbone, Jr., *The Social and Educational Thought of Harold Rugg* (Durham: Duke University Press, 1977).

6. Correspondence of Pauline E. Thompson, 1933, Letter to Erna Bert Nelson, 15 September 1933, Thompson MSS. The first time a folder listed under the Thompson MSS series "Correspondence of Pauline E. Thompson" containing correspondence from a specific year is cited, it will appear in a note; subsequent letters from the same folder will appear as Correspondence followed by a date in the text.

7. Russell's comments are in the Forward to Pauline E. Thompson, *Uncle Sam and Unemployment* (New York City: Bureau of Publications, Teachers College, Columbia University, 1934), in Thompson MSS.

8. "Causes and Effects of Depression Told in Story Book," *New York Post* (Tuesday, 3 April 1934), in Thompson MSS.

9. Pauline was interested in ideas present in communist theory, especially the concept of distributive justice and the question of consciousness. The quote at the beginning of Chapter 2 is from Karl Marx & Frederick Engels, *The Communist Manifesto* (New York: International Publishers, 1948, 1980), 28.

10. "Correspondence, n.d.," Thompson MSS.

11. "Personal Events: Inner-Outer," 1930–1941, Thompson MSS.

12. "Diary Fragment, Relationship with Wilbur," 1931, Thompson MSS.

13. "Abortion," manuscripts, n.d., 45, Thompson MSS.

14. Pauline often changed the names of her lovers in her essays.

15. "Worksheet, Time-line and Analysis of Events," 1905–1950, Thompson MSS.

16. "My Human Relationships, Diary—Bicycle Vacation with Jean Wagner," 21 May to 19 June 1933, Thompson MSS.

17. "She Knew Life and Loved It," March 1996, Thompson MSS.

18. "Protesting," Essay, 29 June 1994, Thompson MSS.

19. Correspondence of Pauline E. Thompson, July–December 1934, Letter to Eugene M. Hinton, 8 December 1934, Thompson MSS.

20. Correspondence of Pauline E. Thompson, July–December 1934 includes a letter from President R. S. Saalfield to P. E. Victory, 15 December, 1934, a letter from P. E. Victory to E. M. Hinton, 18 December 1934, and a letter from E. M. Hinton to P. E. Victory, 23 December 1934.

21. Pauline wrote to her friend Jeannie Wagner, ". . .directing the play was definitely the hardest thing I have ever done. I knew nothing about it, as you know. . ." in Correspondence of Pauline E. Thompson, July–December 1934, Letter to Jeannie Wagner, 2 December, 1934.

22. *Akron Times-Press*, Akron, Ohio, Sunday, 18 November 1934, in Correspondence of Pauline E. Thompson, July–December 1934.

23. Author Interview, May 1997.

24. "Correspondence and Application," Jung Institute, 1951, Thompson MSS.

25. "Memories, Dreams, Reflections," 26 February 1996, Thompson MSS.

26. See Chapter 6 for more on Pauline's views of bisexuality and the feminine.

27. Author Interview, May 1997.

CHAPTER THREE

1. "Where is my Heaven," 22 January 1992, Thompson MSS.

2. Correspondence of Pauline E. Thompson, July–December 1941, Letter to Arthur, 26 September 1941, Thompson MSS.

3. See, for example, Correspondence of Pauline E. Thompson, July–December 1941, Letter to Harold, 25 July 1941.

4. "Correspondence, Letter from A. Minton," n.d., Thompson MSS.

5. "Application for Federal Employment Form," May 1952, Thompson MSS.

6. "Migratory labor camps," 1942, Thompson MSS.

7. "Collected Letters Drafted," October 1943, Thompson MSS.

8. "U.S. Army discharge papers," 14 March 1946, Thompson MSS.

9. "Letter to mother from Hammond General Hospital, Modesto, California," 28 June, 1944, Thompson MSS.

10. Correspondence of Pauline E. Thompson, 1944, Thompson MSS.

11. "Personal Notes and Diary Pages," U.S. Army 1944–1945, Thompson MSS.

12. Dreams and Associations, January-March 1950, 22 February 1950, Thompson MSS.

CHAPTER FOUR

1. Author Interview, September, 2004.

2. "Correspondence from Renée Brand," May–June 1949, Thompson MSS.

3. Dreams and Associations, January–December 1955, 4 March 1955, Thompson MSS.

4. See Dreams and Associations, January–December 1956, Thompson MSS.

5. "Correspondence, January 1952–May 1953," Thompson MSS. The Medical Society is now called the C.G. Jung Institute of San Francisco.

6. See Dreams and Associations, January–December 1957, 9 February 1957, Thompson MSS.

7. Dreams and Associations, June–December 1953, Thompson MSS. The Jung Institute was located at 2206 Steiner St., San Francisco, CA. See "Correspondence and Application."

8. Dreams and Associations, January–June 1953, Thompson MSS.

9. Dreams and Associations, January–December 1955, 6 May 1955.

10. Dreams and Associations, January–December 1955, 7 June and August 1955. Throughout 1955, Pauline had a number of loyal friends who helped her with decisions facing her, about whom and to whom she referred in her writing regularly. She wrote of Hildegaard, a therapist she saw while Renée was away for some months (at times with some envy of Renée's attentions toward "Hilde") (8 August 1955); of Dick, a mutual friend of her and Lee; of Margaret Gibbs Montague; and of friends Eleanor and Wayne (3 October 1955).

11. Dreams and Associations, January–December 1960, 30 June 1960, Thompson MSS.

12. Dreams and Associations, Letter to Renée Brand, 22 January 1961, Thompson MSS.

13. "Saturn," 2 February 1993, Thompson MSS.

14. Carl G. Jung, *Memories, Dreams and Reflections*, recorded and ed. Aniela Jaffé, trans. Richard and Clara Winston (New York: Vintage Books, 1965), 355.

15. Author Interview, May 1997.

16. Dreams and Associations, January–March 1950, Saturday a.m., 11 March 1950. Entries are entitled "My Burdensome Gift of Love" and "Rejection of a School-girl Crush."

17. "Index to Negatives for Active Imagination color painting," n.d., Thompson MSS.

18. Dreams and Associations, August–September 1950, 1 September 1950, Thompson MSS.

19. Dreams and Associations, January–December 1961, 8 December 1961, Thompson MSS.

20. Jung, *Memories, Dreams and Reflections*, 48.

21. Jung, *Memories, Dreams and Reflections*, 50.

22. Dreams and Associations, January–December 1957, 28 November 1957, Thompson MSS.

23. See Dreams and Associations January–December 1955, Tuesday, 15 March 1955; and January–December 1956, 6 December 1956.

24. Dreams and Associations, "My Dreams Dammit Are Like Everything Else — All or Nothing!" 17 October 1972, Thompson MSS.

25. Dreams and Associations, January–December 1962, Letter from Philippines to Renée Brand, 12 December 1962 Thompson MSS.

26. Adrienne Rich, "Transcendental Etude," *Dream of a Common Language* (New York: W.W. Norton, 1978). Pauline's character and penchant for editorial control was evident when I sent a first draft of this manuscript to her. I included Adrienne Rich's poem in the package I sent Pauline. When she returned the draft to me, she had edited Rich's poem.

CHAPTER FIVE

1. "February 1967 letter," Thompson MSS.

2. Christmas letters 1970–1979, Christmas 1977, Thompson MSS.

3. See obituary of Dr. Pauline E. Thompson, *San Francisco Chronicle* (8 December 2000).

4. "Fresh Roses" Christmas Letter 1973, Thompson MSS.

5. Author interview, May 1997.

6. Christmas Letters, 1980–1989, December 1980, Thompson MSS.

7. "My Cross — Undated Christianity," 1995, Thompson MSS. Hereafter noted as "My Cross" in the text.

8. "Getting Arrested," City of San Francisco arrest notice, 14 June 1994, Thompson MSS.

9. "Comfortable," 21 June 1994, Thompson MSS.

10. *The Bellingham Herald*, Bellingham, Washington, Sunday, 19 February 1984.

11. Email from Robert Levering, 13 January 2001.

12. Email from David Hartsough to the author, 11 August 2004.

13. "Getting Arrested in 1987," Thompson MSS.

14. "Runyon/Ego," 11 February 1996, Thompson MSS.

15. "The World is Out of Joint," 14 February, 22 March 1996, Thompson MSS.

16. "A Partial Formulation of my Philosophy," 1978, Thompson MSS. Ironically, as committed as she herself was, Pauline did not expect others to join her activism unless appropriate for them. In 1995 she sat in a rocking chair in my living room, telling

my family and me stories of her antinuclear efforts. At one point my spouse asked her in the face of the enormity of the nuclear threat what he, personally, could do to protest. She paused, then looked up and surprised us by her answer, "Nothing." There is nothing one could do, she explained, as a parent of young children. She felt it was her job, having no children depending upon her, to risk her life for our children's sake.

17. Correspondence of Pauline E. Thompson, January–May 1996, "Diversity," 14 May 1996, Thompson MSS.

18. Christmas letter, December 1996, author's files.

19. In her ninth living decade, between the years 1992 and 1995, Pauline typed out many original theological treatises and musings, as well as committing previous works from the 1950s through the 1990s to computer. In addition, in 1992 she retyped dozens of dream journal entries on her computer. She compiled some 375 drawings and paintings created during her analysis. She had a copy machine in her house and made copies of each entry and drawing for her files.

CHAPTER SIX

1. Author Interview, March 1998.

2. Christmas Letters, 1980–1989, "Party Invitation and Epiphany Greeting," 1981, Thompson MSS.

3. "Right and Left Wing Christians," 1995, Thompson MSS.

4. "My Self as Treasurer," July 1995, Thompson MSS.

5. Author Interview, February 1998.

6. "Paradox," 12 December 1994, Thompson MSS.

7. "Opposites, Number Two: Duality, Yang/Yin, Lost Eden," April 1994, Thompson MSS.

8. "I Ching," March 1996, Thompson MSS.

9. "Know Thy Self," 1995, Thompson MSS.

10. Christmas letter, December 1996, author's files. Pauline wrote yearly letters to her friends containing such words of wisdom. The quote at the beginning of Chapter 5 is found in her 1973 Christmas Letter entitled "Fresh Roses," and was also reprinted in the "Friends Bulletin" (vol. 51, no. 6) of the Pacific and North Pacific Yearly Meetings of the Religious Society of Friends, March 1983.

11. "Jungian Analysis, Renée Brand," 13 May 1968.

12. "Synthesis," 1995, Thompson MSS.

13. Ann Kreilkamp, "Facing the End as A New Beginning: Where The Fire And The Rose Are One: Crone Chronicles discovers Dr. Pauline E. Thompson," in *Crone Chronicles: A Journal of Conscious Aging* 44:(Autumn Equinox 2000) 20.

14. "The Only Dance There Is, by Ram Dass," August 1995, Thompson MSS.

15. "Being and Becoming," 13 February 1992, Thompson MSS.

16. "Party Invitation and Epiphany Greeting," 1997, author's files.

17. "Philosophy/Contributions," undated, Thompson MSS.

18. "Aquarian Age—Wisdom," 1995, Thompson MSS.

CHAPTER SEVEN

1. "My Whole Life," 27 December 1994, Thompson MSS.

2. Carl G. Jung, *Psychological Types,* rev. R. F. C. Hull, trans. H. G. Baynes (Princeton: Princeton University Press, 1971), 460; see also 330–486.

3. See editor's note, Jung, *Psychological Types*, 460.

4. Andrew Samuels, Bani Shorter and Fred Plaut, *A Critical Dictionary of Jungian Analysis* (New York: Routledge, 1986), 155.

5. P.E.T. Exhibit, MASC, April–May 1994, Thompson MSS.

6. "Letter to Friends," 4 July 1995, Thompson MSS.

7. Scotty McLennan, *Finding Your Religion* (San Francisco: Harper San Francisco, 1999). See also Lawrence Kohlberg, *The Philosophy of Moral Development* (San Francisco: Harper & Row, 1981); and Jim Fowler and Sam Keen, *Life Maps* (Waco, TX: Word Publisher, 1978).

8. See Thomas Keating on developing an intentional awareness of God's presence in *Open Hands, Open Heart* (New York: Continuum, 2001).

9. Carol Gilligan, *In a Different Voice* (Cambridge: Harvard University Press, 1982). See also Virginia Held, *Feminist Morality* (Chicago: University of Chicago Press, 1993); and Sarah Ruddick, "From Maternal Thinking to Peace Politics," in *Explorations in Feminist Ethics,* ed. Eve Browning Cole and Susan Coultrap-McQuin (Bloomington: Indiana University Press, 1992), 141–55.

10. Gilligan herself asks this question in "Remapping the Moral Domain: New Images of Self in Relationship," in *Mapping the Moral Domain*, ed. Carol Gilligan, Janie Victoria Ward, and Jill McLean Taylor (Cambridge: Harvard University Press, 1988).

11. Many theorists have tackled these issues. See Joan Scott, "Deconstructing Equality-Versus-Difference: Or, the Uses of Poststructuralist Theory for Feminism," in *Conflicts in Feminism*, ed. Marianne Hirsch and Evelyn Fox Keller (New York: Routledge, 1990), 134–48, on the historical construction of motherhood; Joan Williams, "Deconstructing Gender," in *Feminist Legal Theory*, ed. K. Bartless and R. Kennedy, (Boulder, CO: Westview, 1989), 95–123, on the economic marginalization of women and the "ideology of domesticity"; Linda Kerber, "Some Cautionary Words for Historians," in *An Ethic of Care*, ed. Mary Jeanne Larrabee (New York: Routledge, 1993), 102–107, on the nineteenth-century "cult of true womanhood"; Elizabeth Spelman, *Inessential Woman* (Boston: Beacon, 1988), on power dimensions between women; and Judith Butler, "Gender Trouble, Feminist Theory and Psychoanalytic Discourse," in *Feminism/Postmodernism*, ed. Linda J. Nicholson (New York: Routledge, 1990), 324–40, on challenges to psychoanalytic theory itself as presuming and enforcing heterosexuality with its two gender possibilities.

12. I Timothy 2:11, Revised Standard Version. H. Richard Niebuhr, *The Responsible Self* (San Francisco: Harper, 1963), 48, equates "virtue" with "manliness." For challenges to this formulation, see Mieke Bal, "Sexuality, Sin, and Sorrow: The Emergence of the Female Character in Women," in *Gender, Religion: A Reader*, ed. Elizabeth A. Castelli (New York: Palgrave Press, 2001), 149–73; Nancy Jay, "Sacrifice as Remedy for Having Been Born of Woman," in Castelli, *Gender, Religion,*

174–94; and Delores Williams, *Sisters in the Wilderness: The Challenge of Womanist God-Talk* (Maryknoll, NY: Orbis, 1993).

13. Elizabeth Cady Stanton and the Revising Committee, *The Woman's Bible* (1895; repr. Seattle: Coalition Task Force on Women and Religion, 1990).

14. Stanton, *The Woman's Bible*, 131.

15. See Valerie Saiving, "The Human Situation: A Feminine View," in *Womanspirit Rising*, ed. Carol P. Christ and Judith Plaskow (San Francisco: Harper, 1979), 25–42, on pride as "negation of self." See also See Sharon Welch, *A Feminist Ethic of Risk* (Minneapolis: Fortress, 1990); Emilie Townes, *Breaking the Fine Rain of Death* (New York: Continuum, 1998), who discusses ethics and the public health crisis among African American communities; and the work of Christian ethicist Beverly Wildung Harrison.

16. Mary Daly, *Beyond God the Father* (Boston: Beacon, 1973), 19. Rosemary Radford Ruether notes masculine images of God become an agent in the sacralization of patriarchy in *Sexism & God-Talk: Toward a Feminist Theology* (Boston: Beacon, 1983), 61.

17. Jung, *Psychological Types*, 359.

18. "Album Cover," 10 September 1993, Thompson MSS. See Jung, *Psychological Types*, 21–23.

19. See Rita Nakashima Brock and Rebecca Ann Parker, *Proverbs of Ashes: Violence, Redemptive Suffering, and the Search for What Saves Us* (Boston: Beacon Press, 2001).

20. Elaine Pagels, *Beyond Belief: The Secret Gospel of Thomas* (New York: Random House, 2003), 33. Pagels also notes that early gnostic followers of Jesus actually identified themselves with God (75). In that sense, Pauline does not mirror the early Gnostic Christians, although coming to know God for her was a process of experience and, finally, of knowledge.

21. Author Interview, April, 1997.

22. Barbara Babcock reviews the work and life of Ruth Benedict and notes that Benedict was aware that it was not fully possible for a researcher to be impersonal in ethnographic work in "'Not in the Absolute Singular': Re-Reading Ruth Benedict," *Frontiers: A Journal of Women Studies* 12:3(1992): 39–78. See also Clifford Geertz, *Works and Lives: The Anthropologist as Author* (Stanford: Stanford University Press, 1988), 139, where he characterizes ethnography as dreamt up by a researcher.

23. Helen Callaway discusses reflexive anthropology in "Ethnography and Experience: Gender Implications in Fieldwork," in *Anthropology and Autobiography*, ed. Judith Okely and Helen Callaway (New York: Routledge, 1992), 33, 45, as does Judith Okely in the same anthology, "Participatory Experience and Embodied Knowledge," 24. For examples of reflexive anthropology see Karen McCarthy Brown, *Mama Lola: A Vodou Priestess in Brooklyn* (Berkeley: University of California Press, 1991); and Ruth Behar, *Translated Woman: Crossing the Border with Esperanza's Story* (Boston: Beacon Press, 1993).

24. In a previous article, I argued that the moral agency of the subject is a critical element often missed when discussing subjectivity and reflexivity in life history research. Gail J. Stearns, "Reflexivity and Moral Agency: Restoring Possibility to Life History Research," *Frontiers: A Journal of Women Studies* 19:3(1998): 58–71.

25. One of the first things I did as I began this project was to elicit permission from Pauline that my work would in no way resemble that autobiographical attempt, and to come to agreement that her autobiography could not be published as it so lengthily stood.

26. My question to her prompted a search that included leafing through piles of papers under her bed, and a visit to a rented storage compartment across town the next day. Pauline did eventually find a box of Wilbur's letters. She was then insistent that a detail such as finding the letters would have a profound altering effect on this book—an example of the way Pauline could make meaning out of a seemingly small event. I admit it did steal some thunder away from the assertion I held until then of her self-centeredness.

27. Author field notes, May 1997.

28. See Figure 4. When Pauline read a draft of this paper, she indicated she had never seen a Spirograph, but was enthusiastically ready to create one and patent it. She utilized a compass in drawing some of her active imagination images. My son, John, brought his Spirograph when he accompanied me on a visit to Pauline in the summer of 1999 and gave it to her. She was delighted when he demonstrated its capabilities.

29. "Memory and Change," September-October 1993, Thompson MSS.

30. This passage is from the essay entitled "Bertha Myself," in which Pauline tells about Bertha, a symbol of herself. Here, I have substituted the term "Bertha" with "myself."

CONCLUSION

1. "Journey's End, re: the Fourth Arm of the Cross," June 1995, Thompson MSS.
2. "Social Anger," March 1996, Thompson MSS.
3. Tillie Olsen, "Tell Me A Riddle," *Tell Me A Riddle* (New York: Delta, 1956), 68.
4. "The Three Marys-and the Fourth (John)," 27 May 1994, Thompson MSS.
5. A selection of works in which Pauline has been featured include a video in which Susan Bostrom-Wong interviewed Pauline in 1992, Bostrom-Wong and Thomas Dunn Richardson, 25 April, 1992, Thompson MSS. Her work has been published in *Parabola,* a magazine of myth, tradition, and the search for meaning. A chapter in Kenneth R. Lakritz and Thomas M. Knoblauch, *Elders on Love: Messages Regarding the Consciousness, Cultivation, and Expression of Love* (New York: Parabola, 1999), 166-88, features Pauline's views on the topic and centrality of love. The article by Ann Kreilkamp in *Crone Chronicles: A Journal of Conscious Aging* written in Pauline's 95th year was a publication which pleased Pauline very much.
6. Author Interview, San Francisco, January 2001.
7. "Silence-Weil," original date unknown, edited 1 July 1992, Thompson MSS.

Index

abortion, 24–28, 32
active imagination drawings. *See*
    Jungian analysis
Aldebaran, myth of, 12–13, 51
American Psychological Association, 49
Analytical Psychology Club of San
    Francisco, 49
Anderson, Kay, 107, 110–11
arrests, of Pauline. *See* civil
    disobedience
astrology, 80, 81, 82–85
atonement. *See* theology of Pauline

Bassett, Lu, 45–48, 50, 51–52
Bellevue Hospital, New York, 33–34,
    106
Bellingham, Washington, 63–64,
    66–68
Berkeley Public School System, 47–49
Bertha, Pauline's dream of, 56–58, 62,
    73
bisexuality. *See* sexuality
Boys High School, Brooklyn, New York
    City, 34, 38, 42–43
Brownson, Carol, 47, 85, 105, 109,
    115n3
Brand, Renée, 7, 47, 50–51, 66;
    Pauline's writings to, 21–22, 48,
    52–55, 59–61

California School for the Blind, Daly
    City, 49–50
California State Psychological
    Association, 49
Cheney State Normal School, 22
Christianity, 95–97; Gnostic
    Christianity, 67, 74, 97; Jesus, 17,
    73–78, 82–83, 97; the Judeo-
    Christian tradition, 67, 74–75; Mary,
    mother of Jesus, 81; Methodist
    Church, Pauline's roots, 7, 56, 74,
    95; and morality, 99; Pauline's
    beliefs, x-xi, 1, 56, 71, 95–97;
    Quaker, 2, 66–71, 76, 109–11; right-
    and left- wing, 75–76, 91; and
    Sophia, 81. *See also* feminine, God,
    metaphors, Pagels, paradox, religion,
    theology
civil disobedience, xvi, 67–71, 105, 110
class. *See* politics of race, women's
    issues
Colville, Washington, 8–12
Communism. *See* politics
cross of Christ. *See* theology

Daly, Mary, 95
democracy. *See* politics
dissertation, Pauline's, 38, 41, 42
duality. *See* paradox and duality

ego. *See* Jung's ideas
Estes, Louisa J., 7, 114n6
ethic of care. *See* feminist ethics
ethnographic research, 97–102

faith development theory. *See* moral
    development theory
feminine, Pauline's concept of: and God,
    79, 81, 83, 95–97; as a new future
    path, xi; 80–83; virtue and
    Christianity, 92–95. *See also* feminist
    ethics, God, sexuality, women's issues
feminist ethics, 92–95
four-star metaphor. *See* metaphors
Friends House, Santa Rosa, California,
    2–4, 114n2

gender. *See* feminine, feminist ethics,
    politics of, sexuality, women's issues
Gibbs, Margaret. *See* Truesdale,
    Margaret
God, Pauline's understandings of, 62,
    70, 75–80, 104–5, 106, 108–9; called
    by, 19–22, 55–57; images and nature
    of, x, 79–80, 81, 83, 91–92, 95–97.
    See also Christianity, feminine,
    Jung's ideas, religion, theology
Gooch, Wilbur, 25–28, 31–33, 99

Hartsough, David, 68–69
heterosexuality. *See* sexuality
Hockenhull, Jo, 106
homelessness. *See* politics
homosexuality. *See* sexuality

Jung, Carl, 47, 51, 60, 96; influence on
    Pauline, 73–74, 87–90; concept of
    psychological types, 89; concept of
    religion, 73; scholars of, 49. *See also*
    Jungian analysis, Jung's ideas
Jungian analysis, 51–62; active
    imagination drawings, 14, *72*, 96,
    100, *102*
Jung's ideas, Pauline's understanding of,
    80; ego, 74, 78, 80, 88;

psychological types, x, 89–90,
    107–9; self, 53, 66, 69, 80, 82–83,
    88, 90; shadow, 51, 58–62, 88;
    synchronicity, 6, 78, 96, 99–100;
    unconscious, 15, 49, 78–80, 83–84,
    88. *See also* religion, theology

Kennedy, John K., wagon train, 6–7
Kreilkamp, Ann, 82, 122n5

Levering, Robert, 68
Livermore Nuclear Facility, 67–68, 71,
    92, 110
Lohmann, Jeanne, 1, 114n2
love, Pauline's concept of, xi–xii, 70,
    74, 78, 85–86, 88, 92, 105, 109–11

marriage. *See* women's issues
Marx, Karl, 19
Massacre Rocks State Park, 7
McGuire, John and Mary Jane, 7
McLennan, Rev. Scotty, 91–92
Medical Society of Analytical
    Psychology, 49, 117n5
Meigs, Frederick, 34–35, 39
metaphors used by Pauline: about
    Christianity, 16, 74; four-stars, 6,
    13–16, 57, 107–9; housework,
    58–59, 62; star image, 5–6, 57, 62,
    74, 85. *See also* Bertha, God, Tao
Methodist Church. *See* Christianity
Migratory Farm Worker's Health
    Program, 44
Montague, Margaret. *See* Truesdale,
    Margaret
moral agency in research. *See*
    ethnographic research
moral development theory, 87–88,
    90–95

New York City, 39, 41, 106. *See also*
    Bellevue Hospital, Teacher's
    College
Nelson, Erna Bert, 12, 23, 28–29, 64
Nelson, Muriel, 14, 63–64, 50

North Central High School, Spokane, Washington, 23
Northwest Business College, Spokane, Washington, 5, 11
nursing, 33–34, 44–47

Olsen, Tillie, 105
Old Trail School, Akron, Ohio, 29–31

pacifism. *See* civil disobedience
Pagels, Elaine, 97, 121n20
Paul, Elizabeth, 7
Paul, Susan Francis Ellis (Zaring), 6
Paul, Thomas, 6–7
Parabola Magazine, 106, 122n5
paradox and duality, Pauline's understanding of, 1, 75, 77–78, 81, 83–84
peace efforts of Pauline. *See* civil disobedience
politics, Pauline's views on, 41–42, 43, 55, 64–65, 71; the Communist Party, 23–24, 29–30, 40–42; democracy, 40–41, 43–44; homelessness, xii, 70–71; racial equality, 70
politics of race, class and gender, 92–95, 98
psychological theory. *See* moral development theory
psychological types. *See* Jung, Jung's ideas

Quaker. *See* Christianity

race. *See* politics, politics of
reflexivity in research. *See* ethnographic research
religion, 53, 56, 90–92; definition of, 73. *See also* Christianity, feminine, God, Jung's ideas, theology
Richardson, Hal, 23
Rich, Adrienne, 61, 118n26
Rognes, Liza, 97
Rosenthal, Pauline, 34
Rugg, Harold, 23, 28

San Francisco, 2, 4, 41, 50, 63, 66, 71, 107
San Francisco Society of Friends House, xv, 109
San Francisco State College, 49
self. *See* Jung's ideas
sexuality, 80–82, 98; bisexuality, 35, 80–81, 93; homosexuality, 33–34, 45–48, 52, 80, 95; heterosexuality, 34, 50, 80, 93, 120n11
shadow. *See* Jung's ideas
sin. *See* theology
socialism. *See* politics: The Communist Party
Spokane, Washington, 5–12, 39, 64
Stanton, Elizabeth and the Revising Committee, 94–95
star image of Pauline's. *See* metaphors
subjectivity in research. *See* ethnographic research
synchronicity. *See* Jung's ideas

Tao, Pauline's mention of, x, xi; Yin/Yang, xi, 88
Teacher's College, Columbia University, New York City, 23–24, 29, 31, 33, 38–41, 84
theology, of Pauline: atonement and the cross of Christ, 77, 82–85, 91, 94, 97; evil, 65–66, 71; evil and God, 75–80; sin, definitions of, 77, 80. *See also* Christianity, feminine, God, religion
Thompson, Edward, 5–11
Thompson, Herbert Melville (Rex), 5, 8, 10, 114–15n11
Thompson, Ida, 5–11, 48
Thompson, Pauline, *xviii, 46*; birth of, 5; childhood of, 5–13, 108; travels of, 41, 50, 61, 63–64. for views, *See also* Christianity, feminine, Jung's ideas, love, religion, theology, women's issues
Truesdale, Margaret, 23, 47, 115n3, 117n10; poetry by, 37, 103–4; letters from Pauline to, 37–38, 39, 40

About the Author

Gail J. Stearns holds an Interdisciplinary doctorate with a focus on gender theory from Washington State University, where she teaches in the Women's Studies Department and the Honors College. An ordained minister of the Presbyterian Church (U.S.A.), she is Director of The Common Ministry at Washington State University, an ecumenical campus ministry organization dedicated to the promotion of spirituality, ethics, justice, and interfaith cooperation.